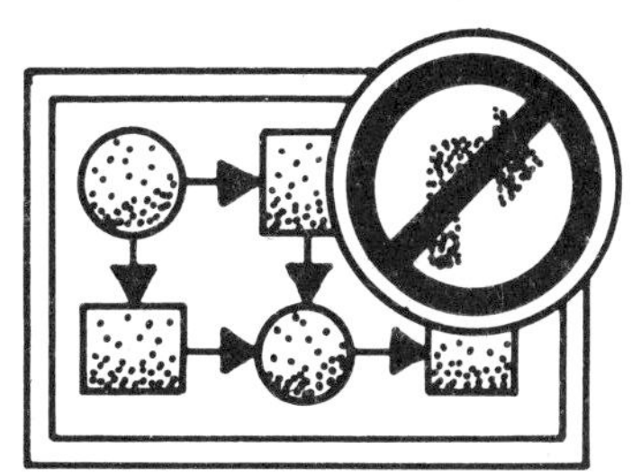

BUILDING VISUAL SKILLS:
Diagrams
and Other Graphic Aids

Grades 2-6

by Linda Ward Beech

SNIFFEN COURT BOOKS/NEW YORK

Artists:
Penny Carter, 8, 10, 13, 15
Maxie Chambliss, 7, 9, 14, 18, 40, 44-46
Ellen Matlach, 11, 16, 17, 19-30, 37, 39, 42, 43, 51, 59, 60, 61
Manuel Rivera, 12, 38, 49, 50, 52-58

Cover Artist:
Maxie Chambliss

ISBN 0-930790-07-3

Printed in the United States of America.

Table of Contents

To the Teacher

Visual literacy is a necessary survival skill in today's society. Furthermore, understanding the visual presentations that accompany any written materials can significantly improve a student's comprehension of the text itself. The reproducible pages in this book provide sequential instruction and ample practice to help students acquire these important visual reading skills.

The activities on these pages are planned to introduce and explain in simple terms a variety of graphic materials. Students are then guided in first finding facts and, subsequently, in using them. Bonus thinking skills, questions signalled by a lightbulb icon, help students interpret, apply, and evaluate information they have identified. Students also have an opportunity to complete many illustrations on the pages and to create their own.

You can use these pages as the basis of discrete skills lessons or as part of another curriculum. The skills covered are applicable to social studies, math, science, language arts, and reading. You will find that the content is lively and relevant to students' interests. The pages are structured so that students can work independently or in cooperative learning groups.

Tips for Use

You may wish to introduce each new diagram or other illustration in a class presentation. Use the instruction call-outs on these pages to help you model thinking for using each type of visual. Students should then be able to work on the following pages independently, in class, or at home. Allow extra time for pages in which students create their own visual materials. In a few cases they will need to do research. For some pages you will need to have colored pencils, markers, or crayons available.

Encourage students, wherever possible, to make up additional questions based on the graphic material. Using the data in this way helps students gain mastery of visual materials. Students can work with partners or in cooperative learning groups for these tasks.

Some bonus questions are open-ended and call for interpretations or opinions. Encourage students to think out their answers and to apply logic. In some instances, you may wish to handle these questions as class discussions.

Two pages at the end of the book review the key elements and related vocabulary covered in *Diagrams*. You may wish to use these pages as a check-up of students' progress.

Ideas for Extension

Encourage students to find and bring in similar diagrams and additional graphic aids from newspapers, magazines, and other publications. Help students see the application to real-life situations.

Many pages lend themselves to an informed discussion. You will want to take advantage of such learning opportunities as they arise.

To emphasize relevance, display those pages that specifically fit in with current topics of study or interest in the class.

Include visual presentations as part of students' assignments for research reports, book reviews, and other papers.

 # Answers

page 7
1. 5; 2. 4; 3. 3; 4. 3

page 8
1. a carpenter; 2. saw; 3. overalls; 4. tools

page 9
1. c; 2. d; 3. f; 4. e; 5. b; 6. a

page 10
Check to see that students have put a kite in the boy's hand, a cloud in the sky, a bench under the tree, TO BIKE PATH on the sign, a picnic basket on the blanket, and another child (or pet) in the picture.

page 11
Check to see that students have followed the picture directions to make a snowflake.

page 12
Check to see that students have followed the directions to start a potato plant.

page 13
1. Now the girl is making a peanut butter and jelly sandwich. Next she will probably eat it. 2. Now the woman is leaving her car parked in a No Parking area. Next she may get a ticket.

page 14
1. the lady in her bathrobe and slippers; 2. the man with an open umbrella; 3. the boy with the lion; 4. the man with the saw; 5. the scarves on the counter; 6. the telephone on the cake; 7. the jewelry in the display case. *None of the items is needed or usually found in a bakery.

page 15
Check to see that students have given logical explanations for the puddle (from the melting ice in the truck which may have stopped at Fred's lunch stand on a hot day).

page 16
1 - 2. Check to see that students have colored the leaves green and the flowers yellow. 3. roots; 4. stem

page 17
1. jib; 2. mainsail; 3. mast; 4. tiller *hull, centerboard, rudder

page 18
1. Check to be sure students circle hackles. 2. Check to be sure students color the comb red. 3. Check to be sure students put an X on the sickles. 4. Check to be sure students underline *saddle*. *six

page 19
1. False; 2. True; 3. True; 4. True *snow, sleet, hail

page 20
1. - 4. Check to see that students label Mercury, Jupiter, Saturn, and Pluto correctly. 5. Venus and Mars; 6. Neptune *The planets nearest the sun are the hottest, and the planets farthest from the sun are the coldest. The sun is the only source of heat for the planets.

page 21
1. dead leaves; 2. rock; 3. subsoil; 4. minerals, topsoil and subsoil

page 22
1. lays eggs; 2. soldier ants; 3. nursery; 4. carry seeds and dig new rooms *The ants eat seeds; they are taking them to the food storage room.

page 23
Check to be sure students identify and circle tower, radar, arresting wires, catapults, and hangar deck on the diagram. *Since the hangar deck is below the main deck, the planes would be moved on the elevators.

page 24
1. two; 2. family room; 3. carport; 4. living room *eleven

page 25
1. porch; 2. living room or kitchen; 3. two; 4. three *Possible answers: couch, chair, lamp, table, bookcase

page 26
1. True; 2. False; 3. False; 4. True *card store

continued on page 63

Eyes on Art

You can read a picture.
Look at each picture on this page.
Then read each question.
Use the pictures to answer the questions.

1. Write the number of striped umbrellas.

   ____

2. Write the number of things that fly.

   ____

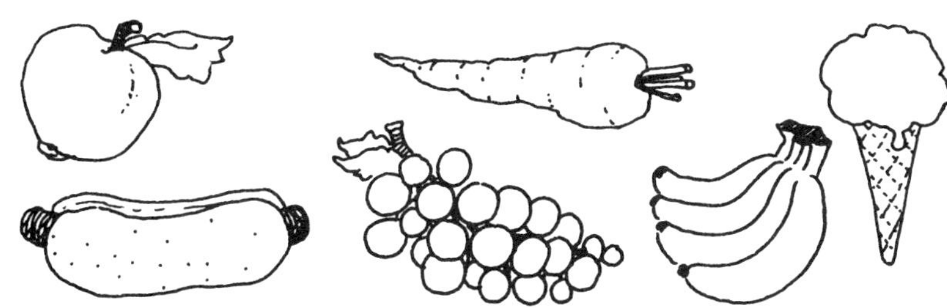

3. Write the number of fruits.

   ____

4. Write the number of wild animals.

   ____

Choose one picture. Make up your own question about it.
Have a classmate answer it.

Get the Picture

You can read this picture.
Then write the answers to the questions.
Use the Word Box.

<table>
<tr><td colspan="4" align="center">Word Box</td></tr>
<tr><td>carpenter</td><td>saw</td><td>nail</td><td>plumber</td></tr>
<tr><td>brush</td><td>suit</td><td>overalls</td><td>tools</td></tr>
</table>

1. Who is working? ___________________________________

2. What does he hold? ___________________________________

3. What is he wearing? ___________________________________

4. What is in the box? ___________________________________

 Write a sentence about the picture.

Picture Places

What can you find in this picture?

The first column names things you see in the picture.
The second column tells where they are.
Draw a line from each thing to the words that tell where it
is in the picture.

Who or What	**Where**
1. Jody	a. behind the mailbox
2. hanky	b. on Jody's feet
3. bird	c. on skates
4. trash can	d. in a pocket
5. skates	e. on the grass
6. squirrel	f. above Jody

Make up three sentences about the picture. Use these words: *in, near, toward.*

The Complete Picture

Someone forgot to finish this picture.
Can you help?
Follow the directions below.

1. Put a kite in the boy's hand.

2. Add a cloud to the sky.

3. Draw a bench under the tree.

4. Write **TO BIKE PATH** on the sign.

5. Put a picnic basket on the blanket.

6. Give the boy a friend.

Color your picture. Then tell about it.

Picture Directions

Pictures can help you make something.
Sometimes pictures are more helpful than words.
Can you make this snowflake?

You will need:

 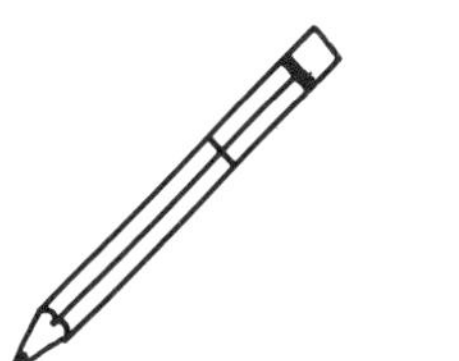 

Do this.

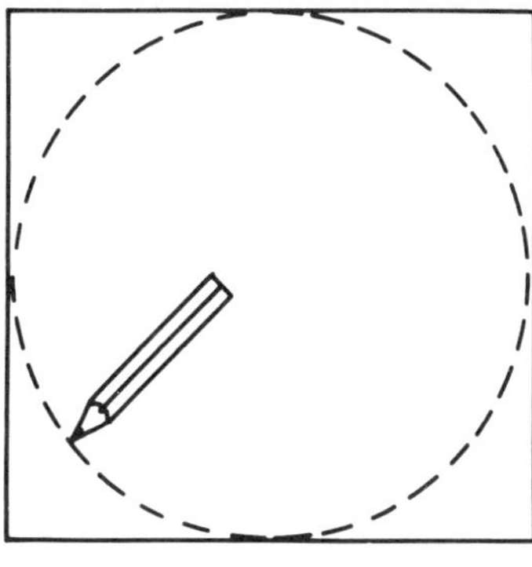 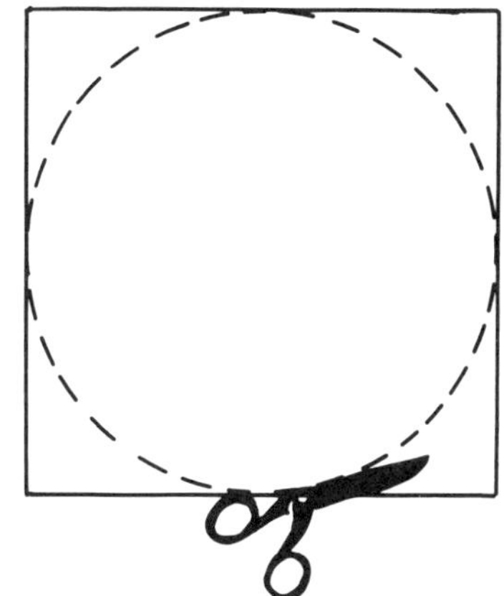 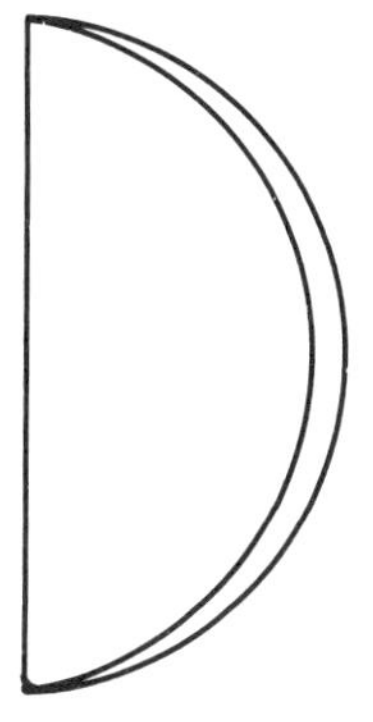 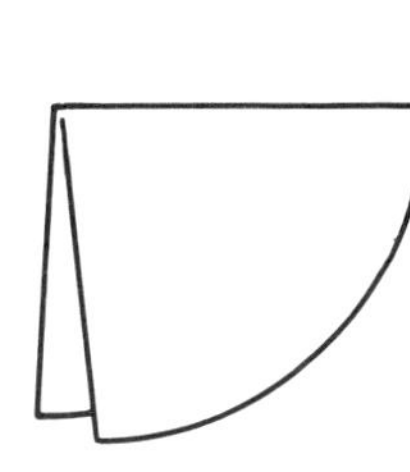

 Write a set of directions to tell how to make a snowflake.

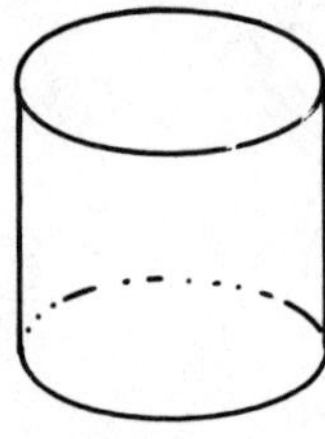

Potato Pictures

Pictures can show you what words tell you.
Read these directions and look at the pictures.
They will tell you and show you how to start a potato plant.

You will need:

glass   toothpicks   sweet potato

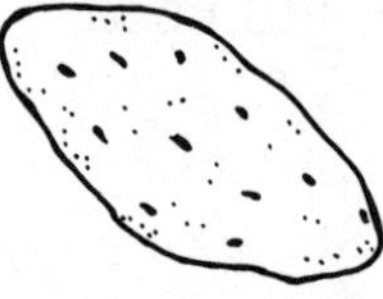

1. Fill glass with water.

2. Stick toothpicks in potato.

3. Place potato in glass.

4. Put glass in sun.

5. Add water as needed.

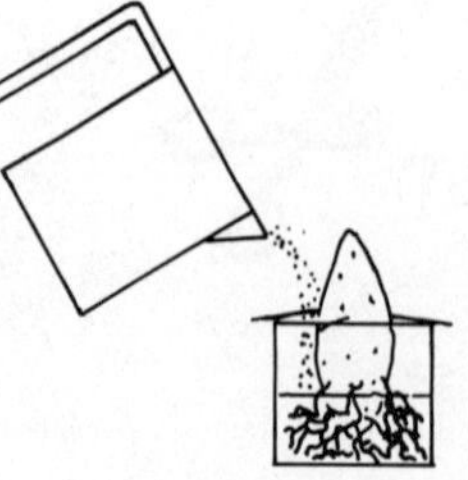

Keep a record of how your potato plant grows. When do you see the first roots? When do you see the first leaves?

Picture Predictions

Pictures often show action. You can see what is happening. You can also **predict**, or make a good guess, about what will happen next.

Study each picture. Write one sentence to tell what is happening. Write another sentence to predict what will happen next.

1. Now ________________________________

____

____

Next ________________________________

____

____

2. Now ________________________________

____

____

Next ________________________________

____

____

Draw a picture to show what you predicted for one picture.

Impossible Pictures

A picture can have mistakes in it. Then you have to be a good detective to spot the mistakes.

Study this picture. Write five things that don't make sense.

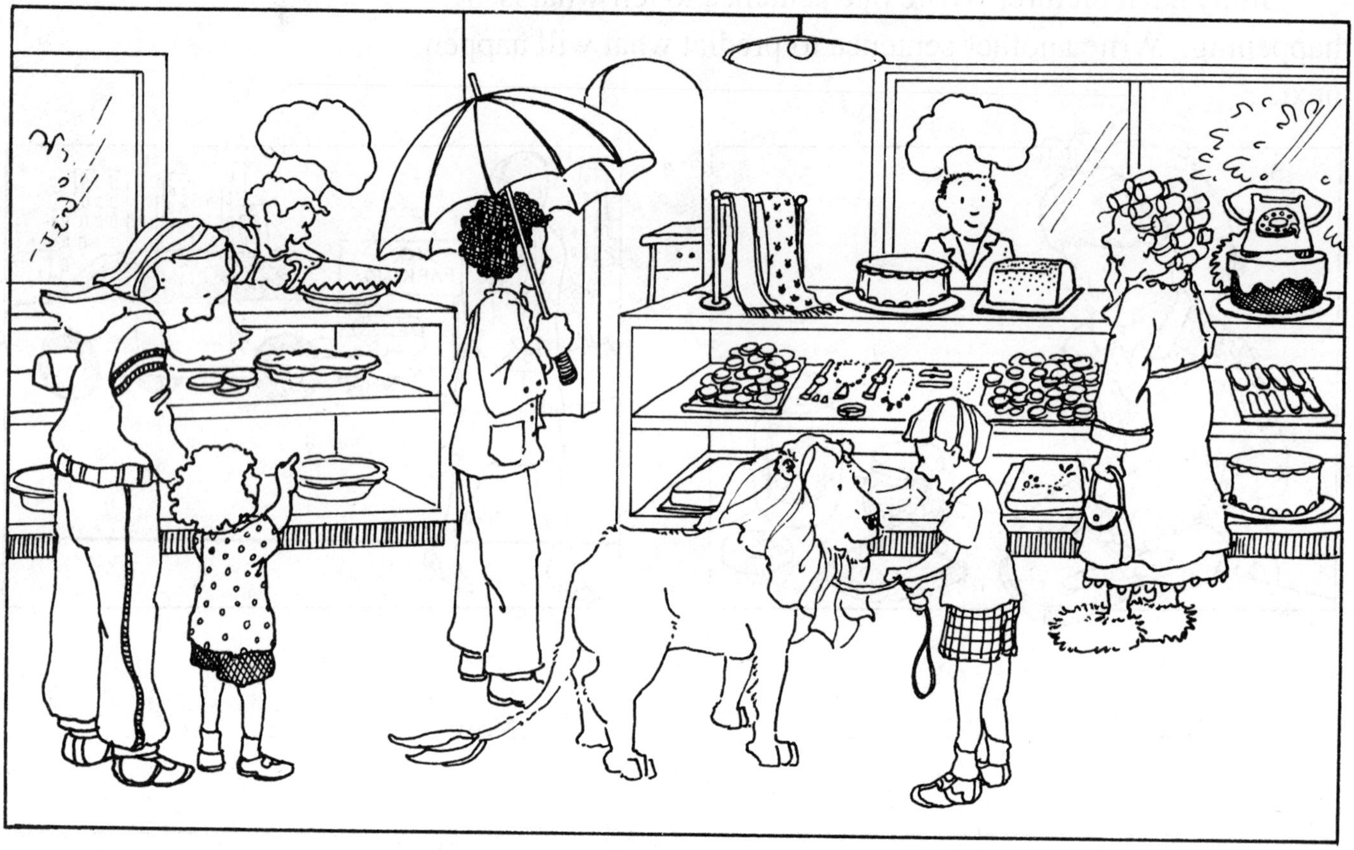

1. ____

2. ____

3. ____

4. ____

5. ____

 Tell how one of the mistakes you found does not fit in.

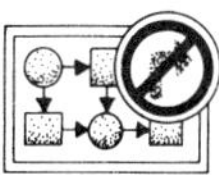

Seeing and Thinking

A picture does not always show you every part of a story. You have to think about what else has happened.

Look at this picture. What has happened? How could you explain it? Write a story below. HINT: Look carefully at the details.

____

____

____

____

____

Compare your story to someone else's. How are they alike? How are they different?

 # Picture Story

A **diagram** is a picture that shows what the parts of things are. This diagram names the parts of a plant. The words on a diagram are called **labels**. The arrows help you see which part of a picture a label tells about.

Read the labels.
Study the parts.

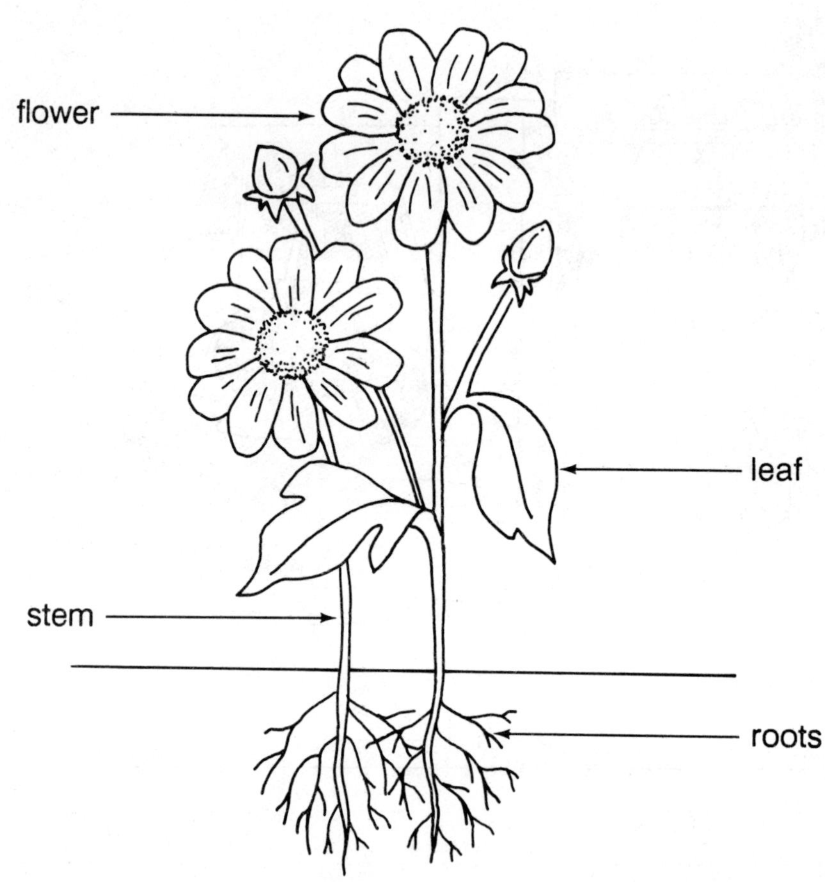

1. Color the leaves green.

2. Color the flowers yellow.

3. What part of the plant is under the ground? ________________________________

4. The leaves grow on the part called the ________________________________ .

Draw a picture of another plant. Label its parts.

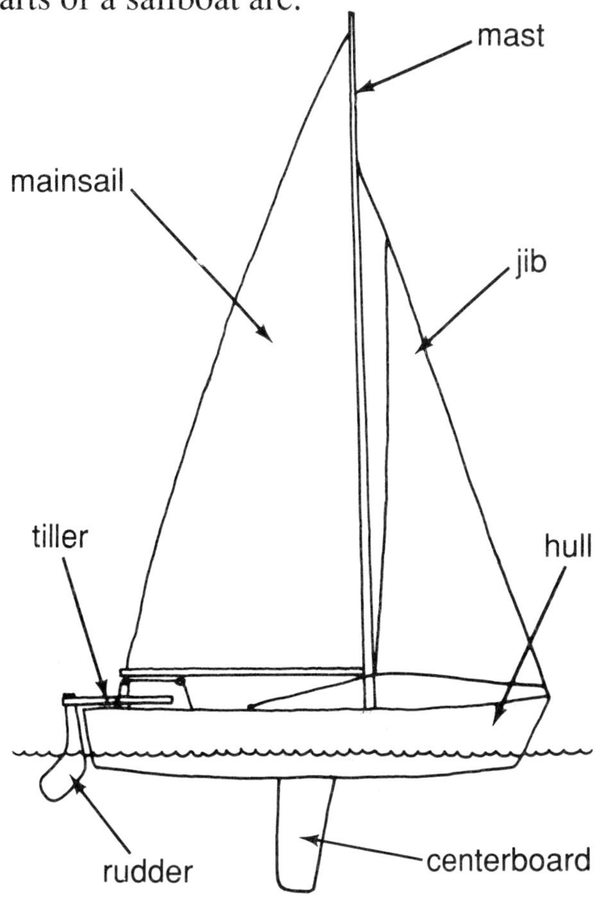 What Is It?

This diagram tells what the parts of a sailboat are.

Study the diagram, then answer the questions.

1. What is the small sail called? ________________________________ .

2. The large sail is called the ________________________________ .

3. A tall pole that holds the sails is the ________________________________

4. You can see that the rudder is connected to a handle

    called the ________________________________ .

Name three parts of a sailboat that are in the water.

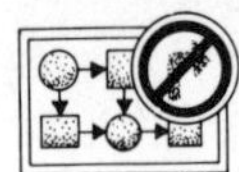

Head to Toe

This diagram shows the parts of a chicken. Study the diagram. Then follow the directions.

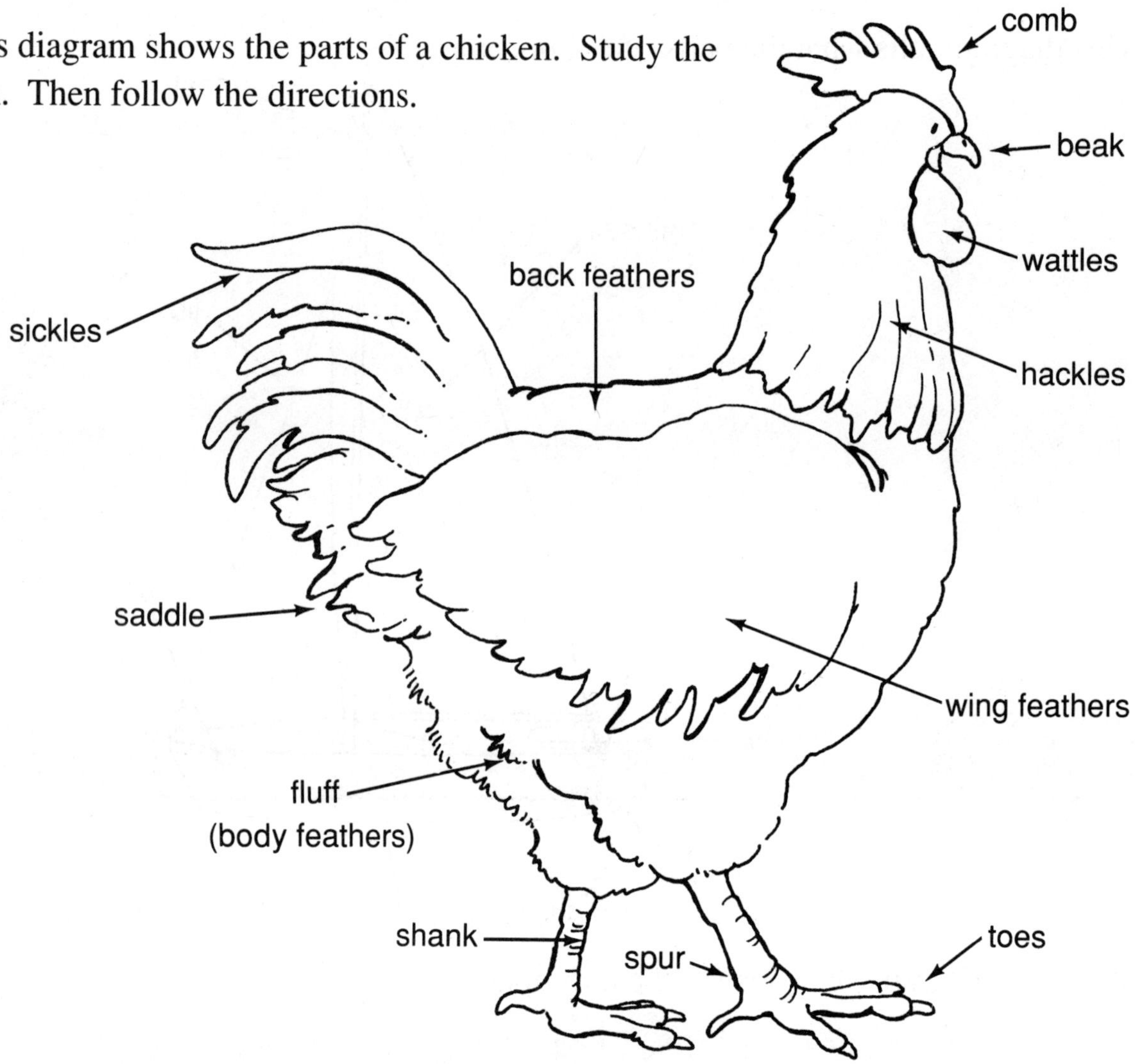

1. Another name for hackles is neck feathers. Circle this label in the diagram.

2. Color the comb red.

3. Sickles are tail feathers. Put an X on them.

4. The rear back feathers make up the saddle. Underline this label.

 How many different kinds of feathers does a chicken have?

How Does It Happen?

What happens to the rain? This diagram shows. Did you know there is always water in the air? It is called vapor. You cannot see vapor.

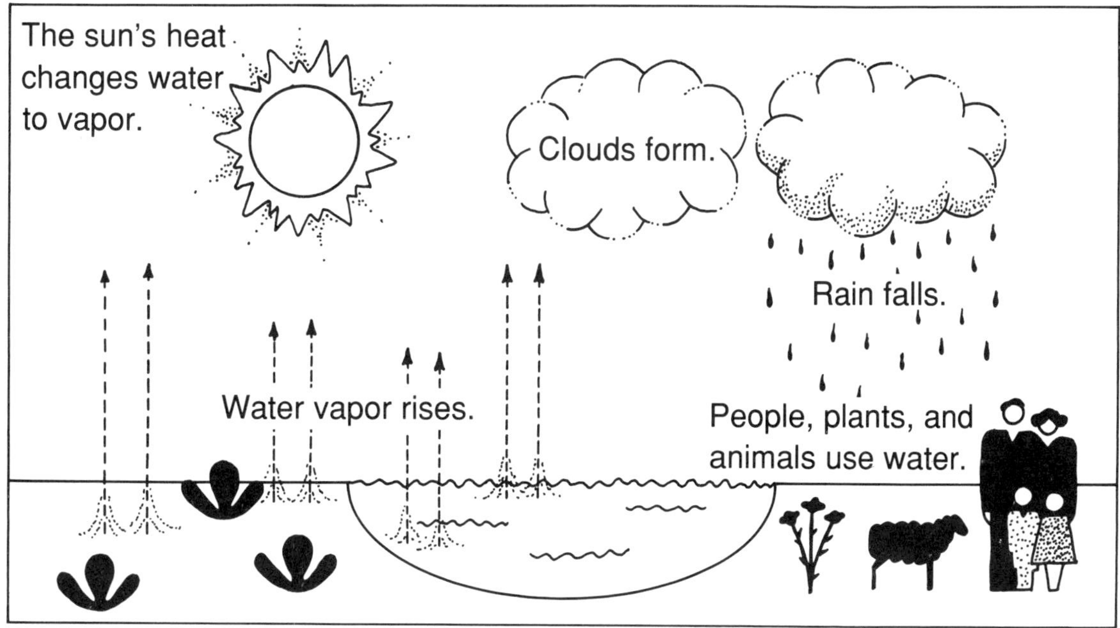

Study the diagram. Then write **True** or **False**.

______________ 1. Animals do not use water.

______________ 2. Rising water is called water vapor.

______________ 3. Rain falls from clouds.

______________ 4. Heat changes water to vapor.

 In what other forms can water fall from clouds?

Name the Planet

This diagram shows the nine planets and the sun. Some of the labels are missing. Follow the directions to add the missing labels.

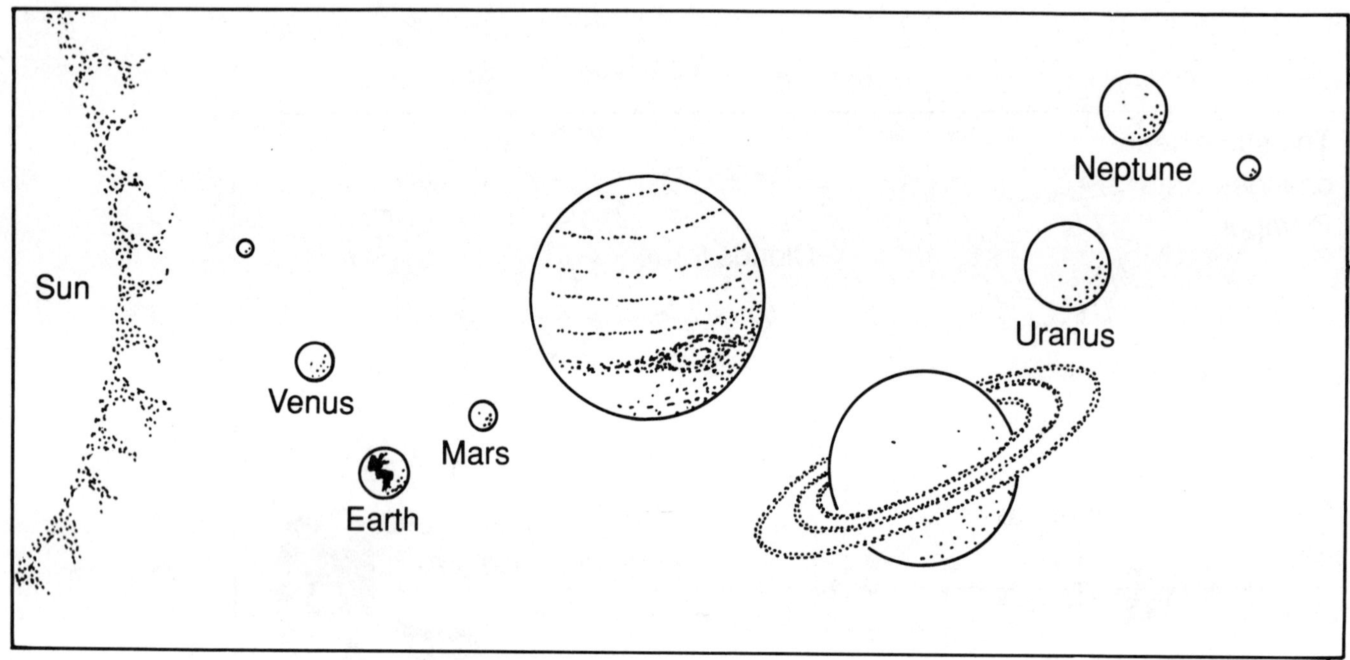

1. The planet nearest the sun is **Mercury**. Label it on the diagram.

2. The biggest planet is **Jupiter**. Label it.

3. **Saturn** has many rings around it. Label Saturn.

4. **Pluto** is the farthest planet from the sun. Label Pluto.

Now, study the diagram, then answer these questions.

5. Name Earth's two closest neighbors. _______________________________

6. Name Pluto's closest neighbor. _______________________________

 Which planets do you think are the hottest? Which are the coldest? Why?

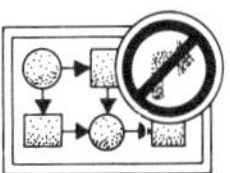

See the Soil

A diagram can show what the inside of something looks like. This kind of diagram is called a **cutaway**. The cutaway diagram on this page shows how soil looks below the ground. It's as if you cut away a slice of earth.

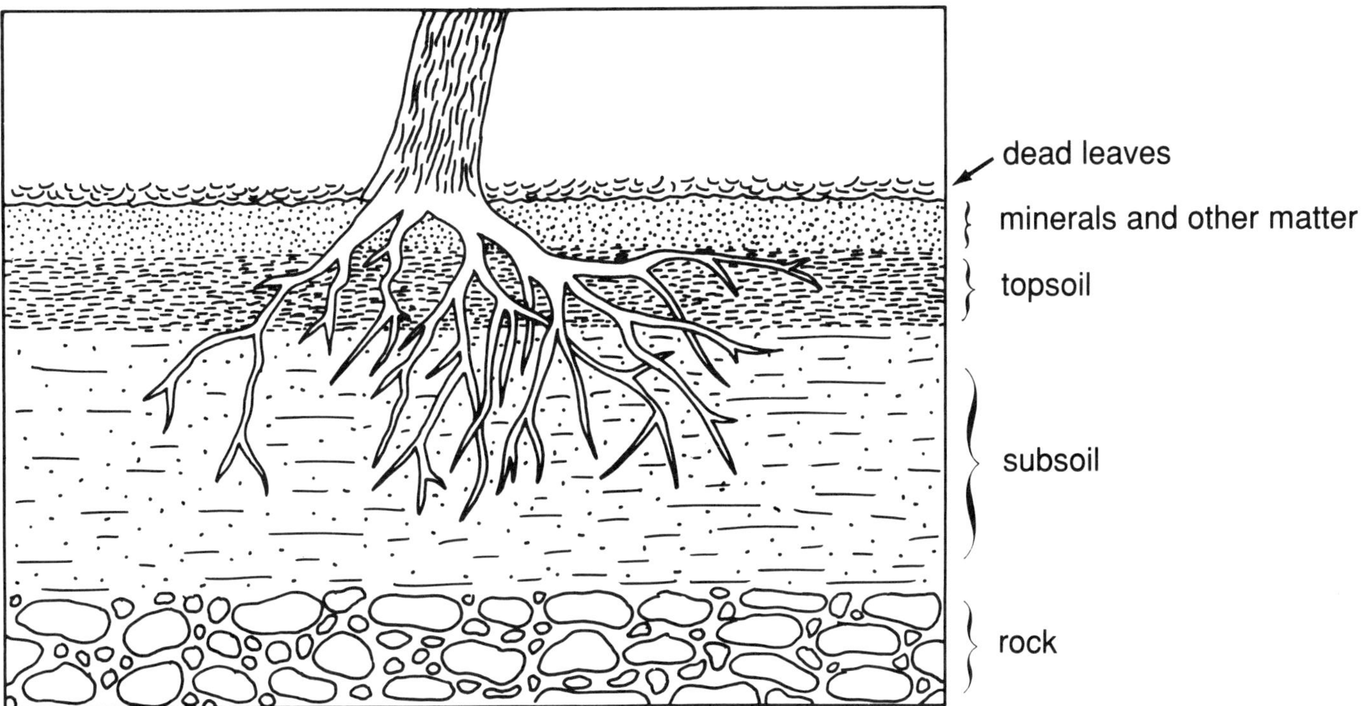

Study the cutaway diagram, then answer the questions.

1. What is in the top layer? ____

2. What is under the subsoil? ____

3. Is the layer of topsoil or subsoil deeper? ________________________

4. Name the layers that the tree roots grow through.

Write a title for the cutaway diagram.

What Goes On?

Have you ever seen an ant's nest? This cutaway diagram shows one.

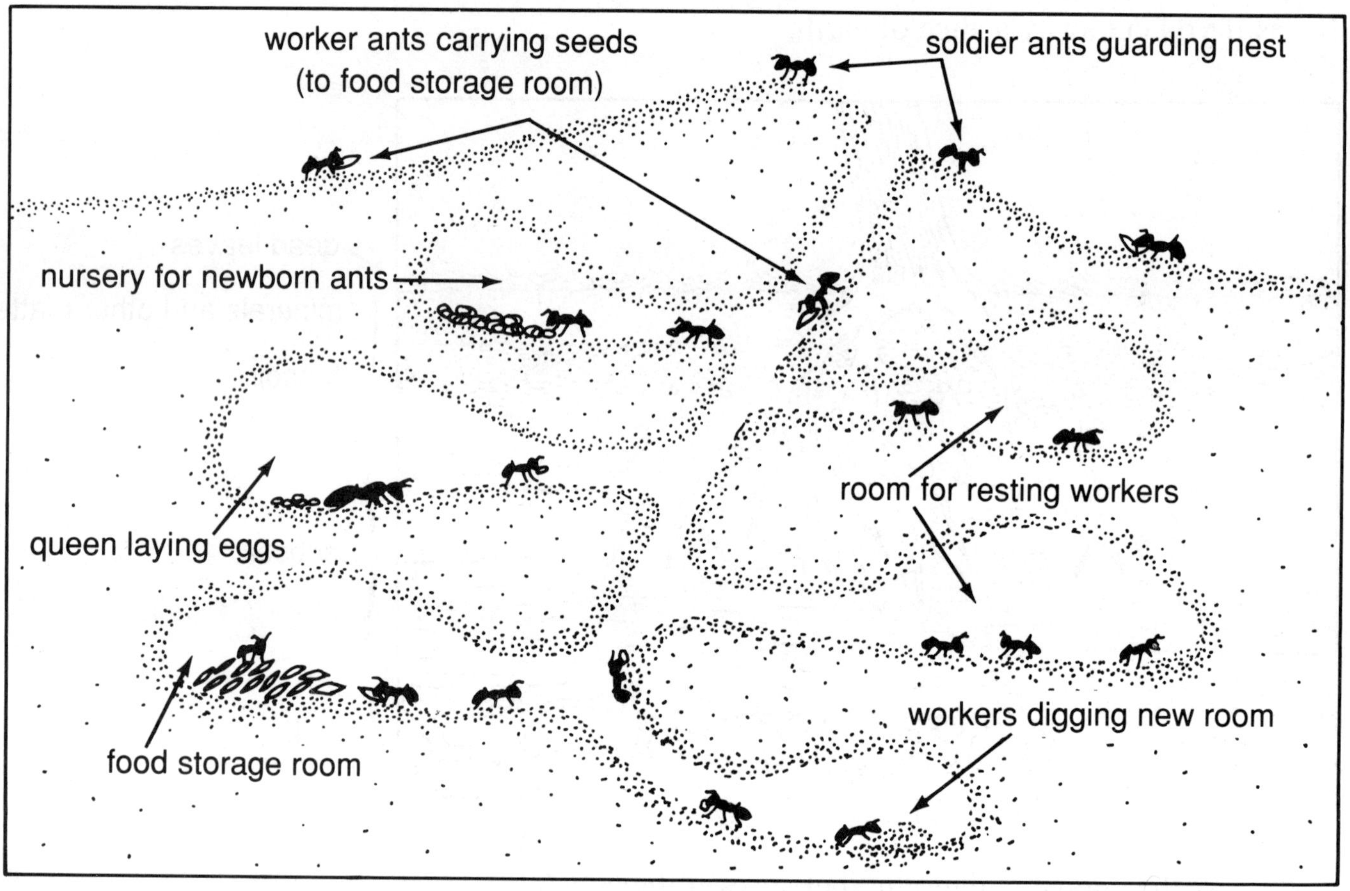

Study the cutaway diagram, then answer the questions.

1. What does the queen do? _______________________________

2. Who guards the nest? _______________________________

3. Where do the newborn ants stay? _______________________________

4. Name two jobs the workers do. _______________________________

 What do the ants eat? How do you know?

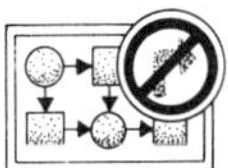

All the Facts

A diagram often helps make your reading clearer. The paragraph below tells how planes take off and land on special ships. The diagram shows such a ship, called an aircraft carrier.

Study the diagram. Read the paragraph. Each time you find a **boldfaced** word, circle it on the diagram.

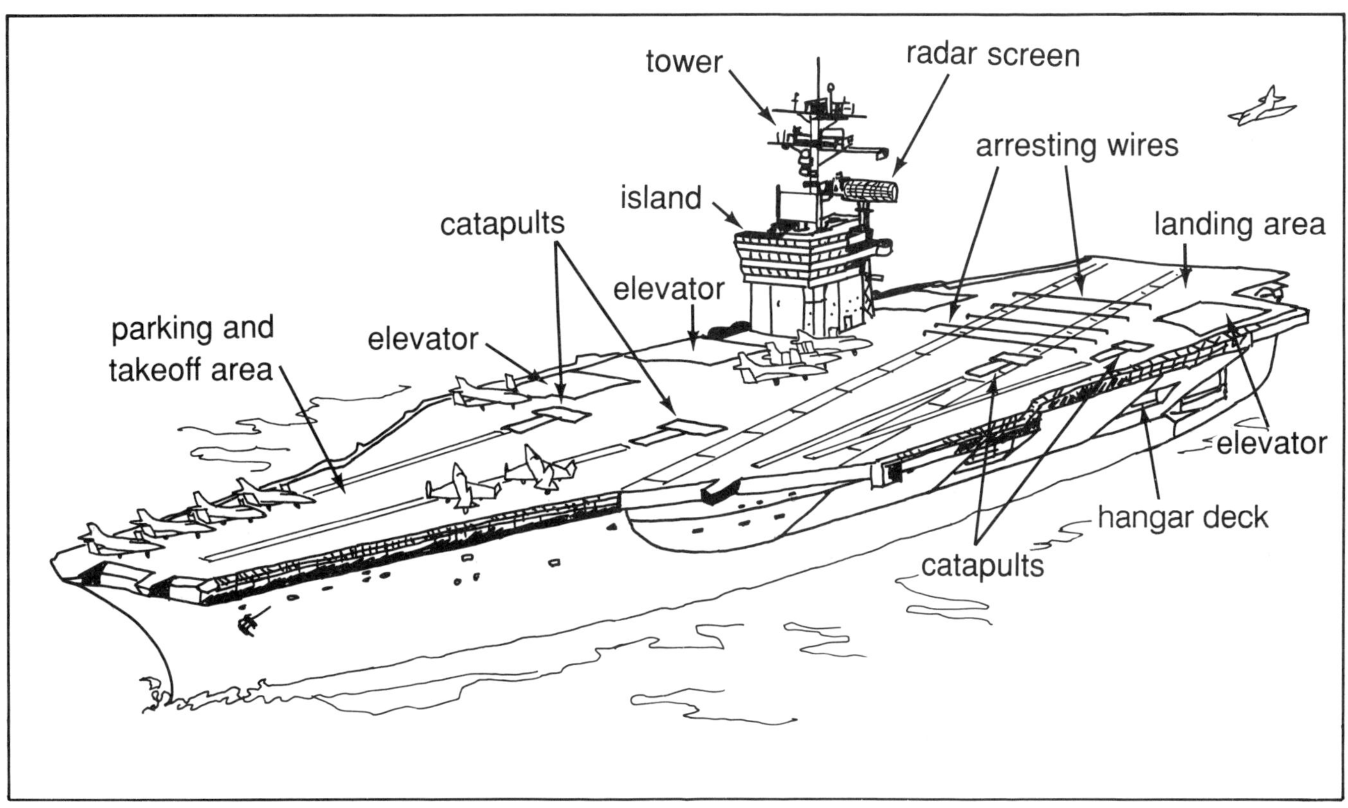

Planes can land on the top of an aircraft carrier. Men in the **tower** use **radar** and other equipment to stay in touch with the pilots. When a plane "hits the deck," **arresting wires** catch it and help it stop. When a plane takes off, **catapults** help lift it into the air. When a plane is not in use, it is stored on the **hangar deck**.

 Study the diagram again. How do you think planes get to the hangar deck?

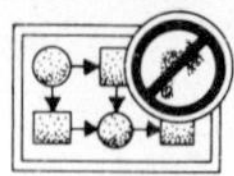

Plan for a House

This picture is a floor plan. A floor plan is like a map of a building. It shows how the rooms are arranged.

Read the labels.

Study the plan.

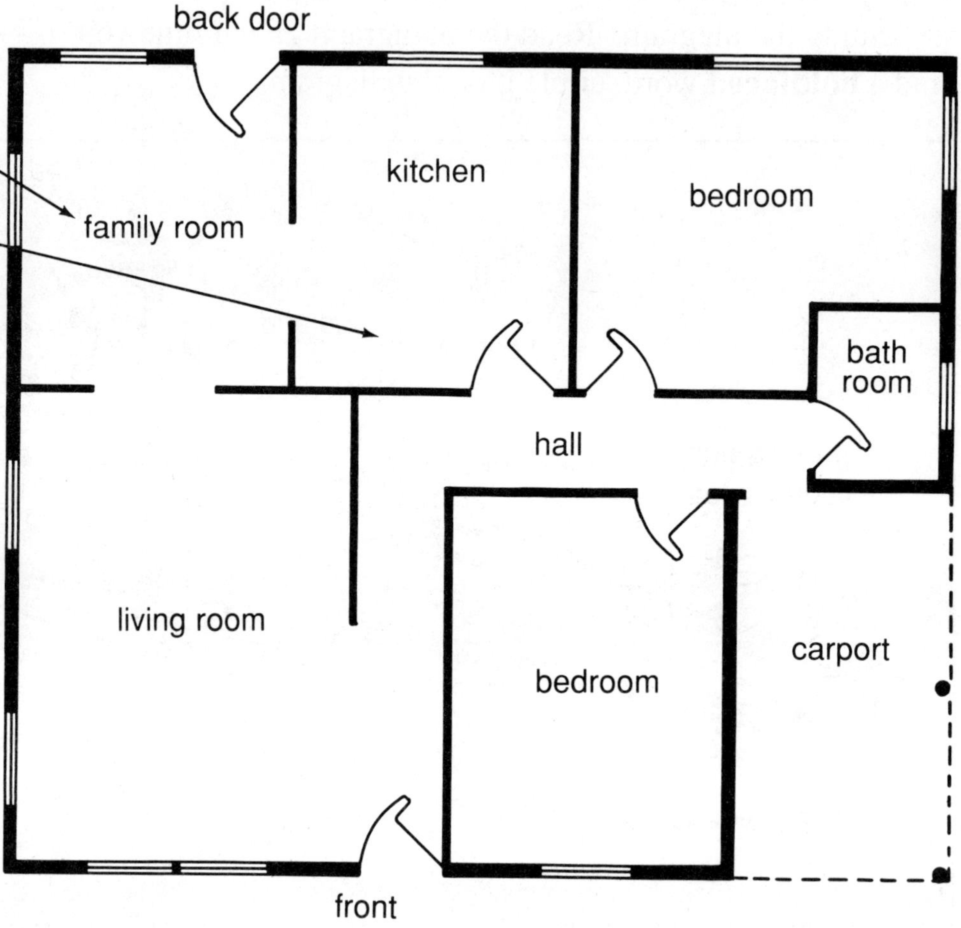

Read the key.

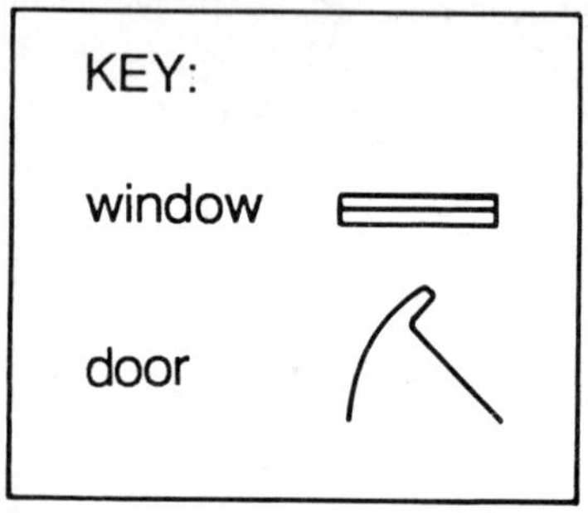

Now, answer the questions.

1. How many bedrooms does the house have? ______________________________

2. What room does not open onto the hall? ______________________________

3. Where could you keep a car? ______________________________

4. What is the largest room in the house? ______________________________

 How many windows does the house have?

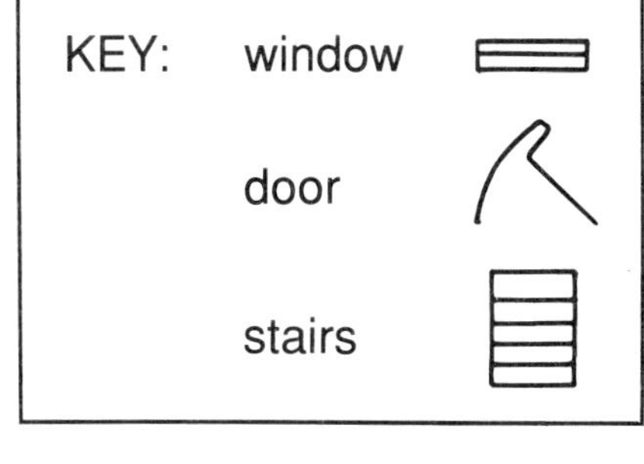

Two Stories

These floor plans show a two-story house.

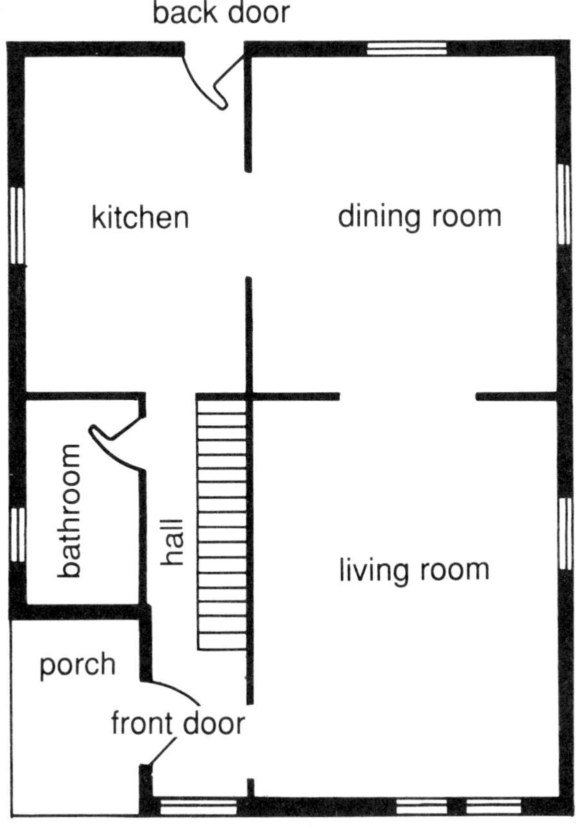

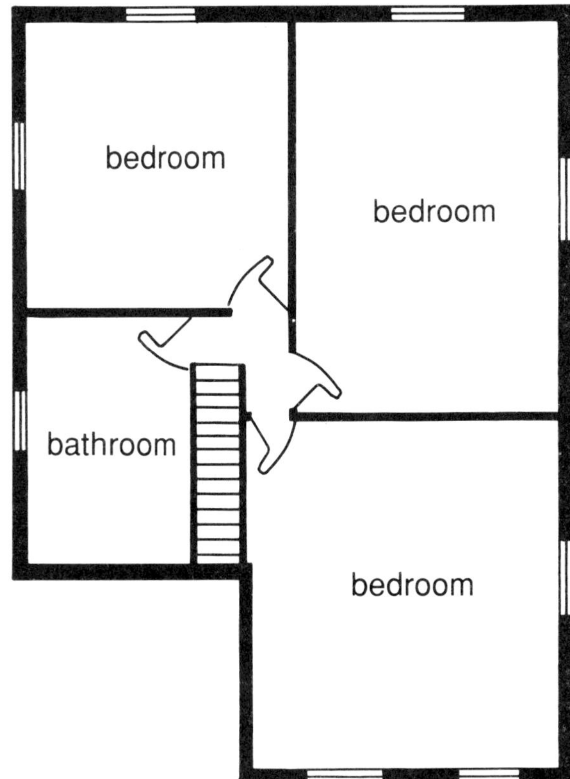

Study the floor plans, then answer the questions.

1. Outside the front door is a ______________________ .

2. To get to the dining room, you have to go through the ______________________

   or the ______________________ .

3. How many bathrooms does this house have? ______________________

4. How many bedrooms does it have? ______________________

Name five pieces of furniture that you would put in the living room.

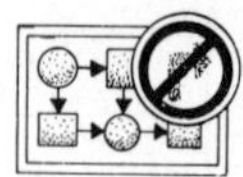 Blum's Blueprint

This a floor plan of a store. It shows where you can find different things for sale.

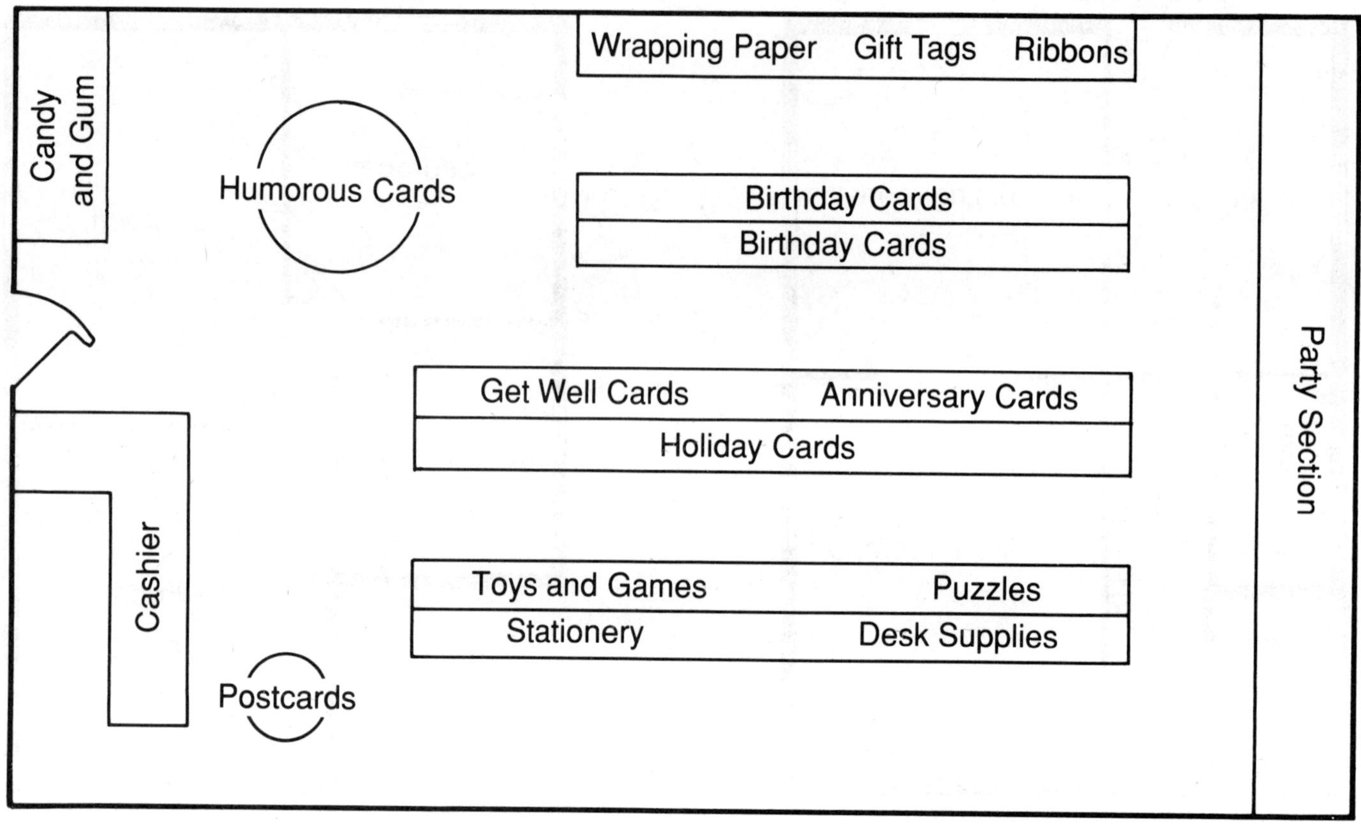

Study the floor plan. Then write **True** or **False** for each statement.

__________   1. If you were planning a party, you might go to Blum's.

__________   2. You could buy a birthday cake at Blum's.

__________   3. The get well cards are next to the wrapping paper.

__________   4. You could probably buy pens at Blum's.

 What kind of store is Blum's?

 # Castle for Sale

This is a floor plan for a castle.

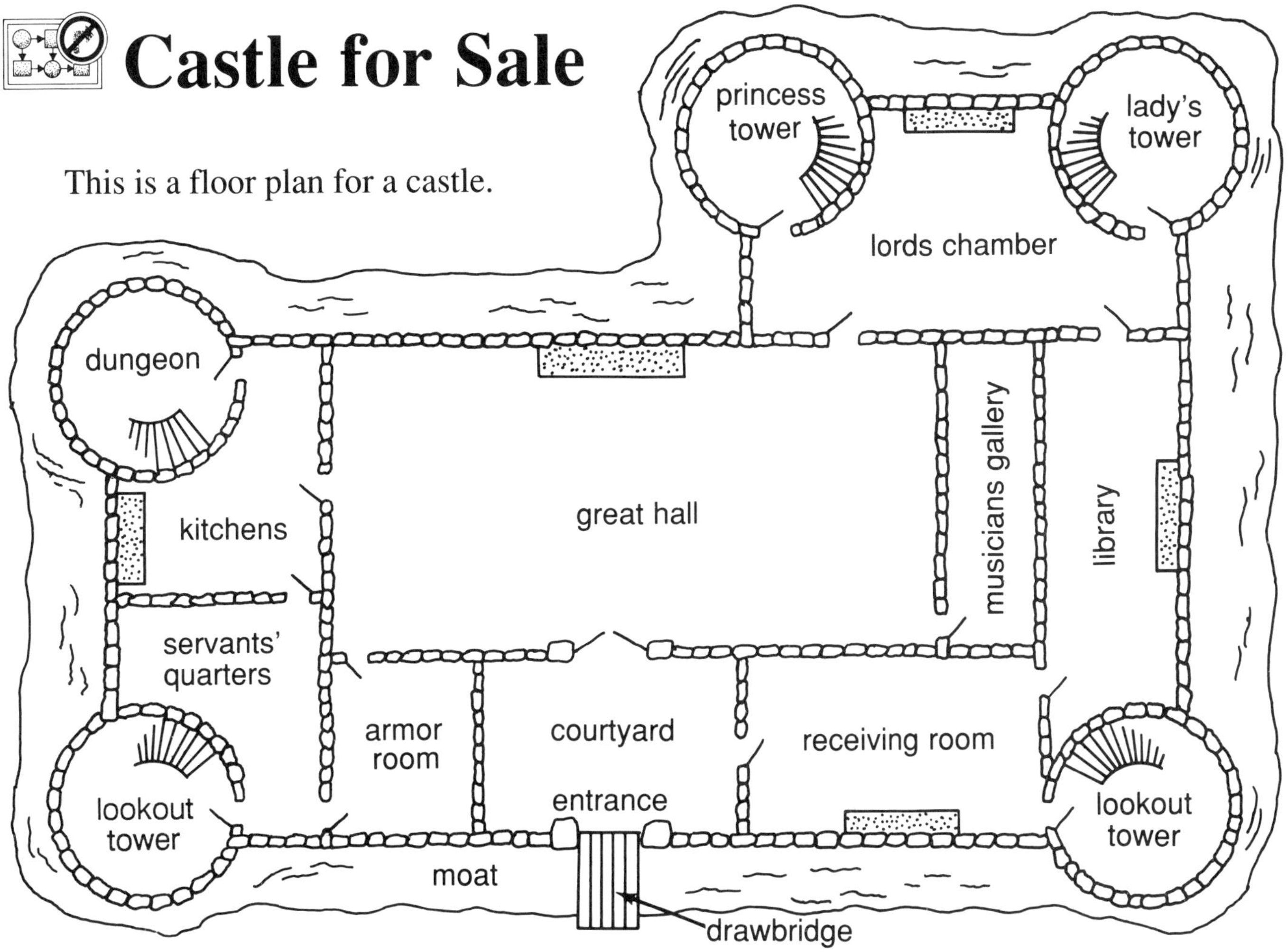

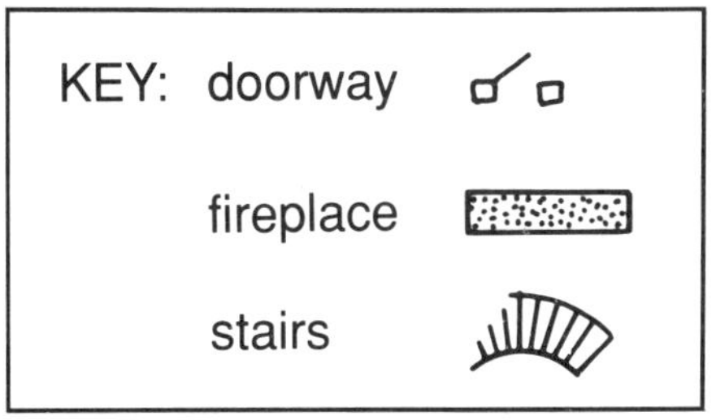

Pretend that you are in the castle business. Study the floor plan, then write an ad to sell this castle.

____

____

____

____

Compare your ad to one that a classmate wrote. How are they alike? How are they different?

 Who's Who Chart

A picture can show how things are organized, or set up. This kind of picture is called an **organization chart**.

The organization chart on this page shows how a class committee is organized. The person in charge is at the top. Lines connect the leader to those below him or her. Lines like this show that two jobs are equal.

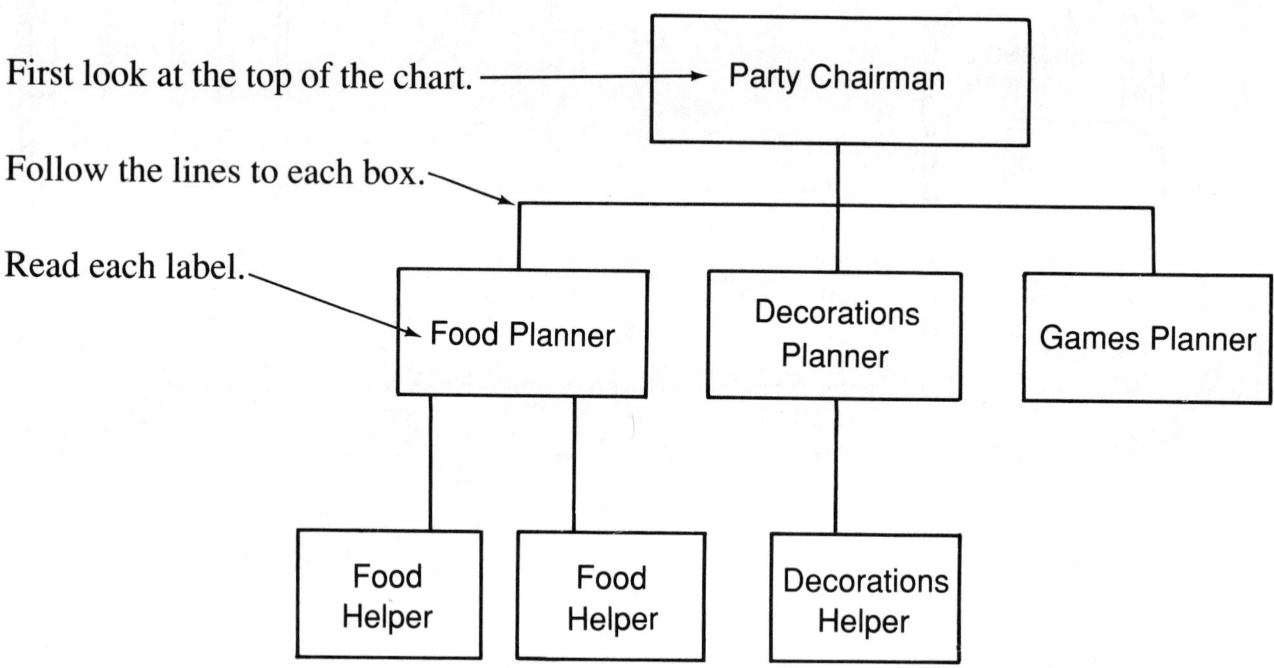

Answer these questions about the organization chart.

1. What is the top job? ___________________________

2. Which job has two helpers? ___________________________

3. Which job has one helper? ___________________________

4. Name three jobs that are equal. ___________________________

What work will this committee do?

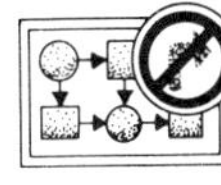 # Chart It

You can organize facts in different ways. Follow the directions to fill out this organization chart.

1. Read the top of the chart.

2. Read the list of state names.

3. Decide which names fit the chart heading.

4. Check your facts. Look up any state names you are not sure of.

5. Write the state names in the boxes.

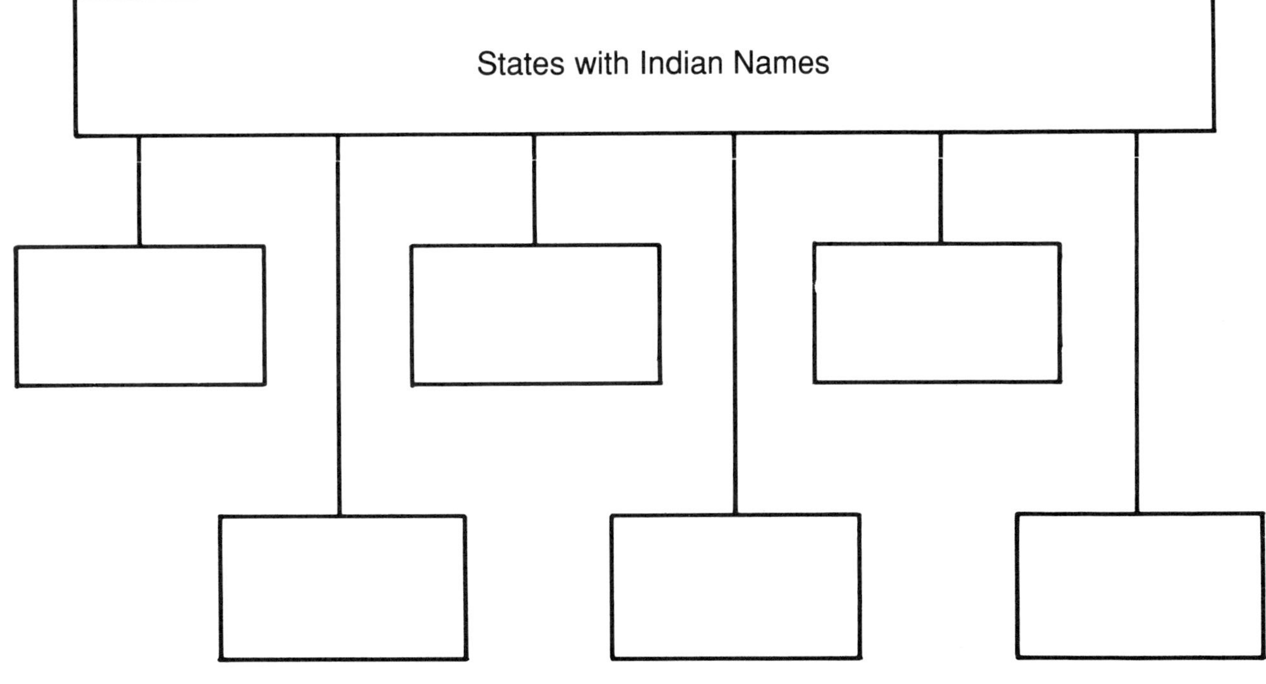

Alabama	Virginia	New York	Massachusetts
Idaho	Mississippi	Washington	Connecticut
Louisiana	Hawaii	Ohio	South Carolina

Find two more states with Indian names. Add them to the chart.

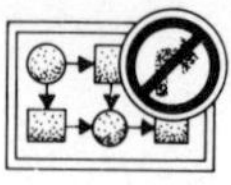

The Order of Things

This chart tells about the food chain in the sea. Start at the top and read down.

Big fish eat . . .

Small fish which eat . . .

Tiny sea animals which eat . . .

Teeny, tiny sea plants

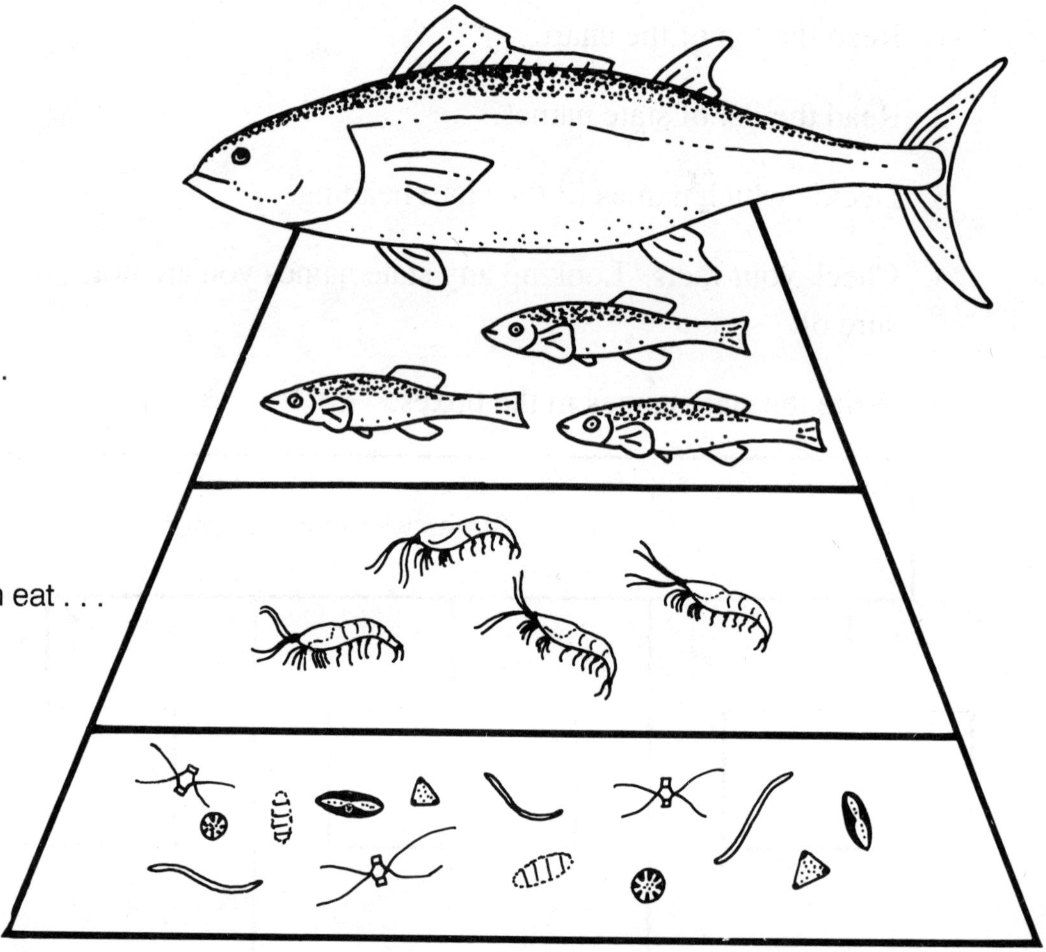

1. What is at the top of the chart? _______________________

2. What do big fish eat? _______________________

3. What do small fish eat? _______________________

4. What eats teeny, tiny sea plants? _______________________

 Where would you put people in this food chain? _______________________

Name ____

 # Ideas on a Map

You can make a map of an idea. This is called an **idea map**. An idea map shows a main idea and some details about it. The idea map on this page is about a garden.

The paragraph below tells about the garden. The main idea is in the center of the idea map. The details are on the lines.

Farmer John has a fine vegetable garden.
In it he has beans, peas, and corn. Carrots grow
in Farmer John's garden, too.

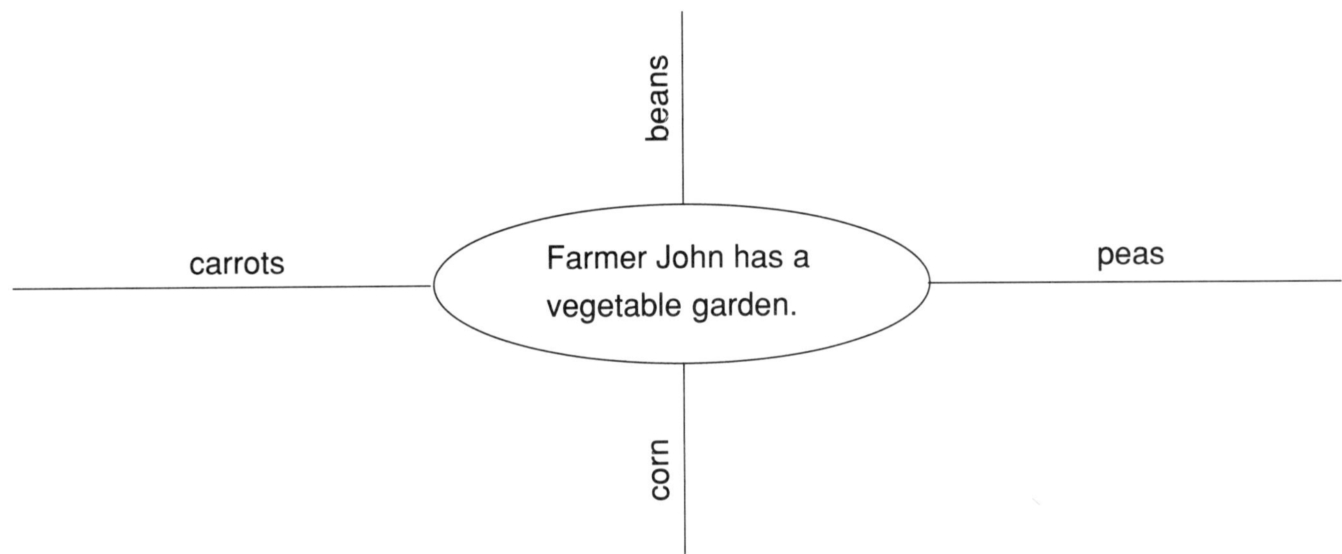

Study the idea map, then answer these questions.

1. What is the main idea? ____

2. Name the details about the main idea. _______________________________

3. Does Farmer John have pumpkins in his garden? _______________________

 Suppose Farmer John also grows beets. How would you
show that detail on the idea map?

Linking Ideas

You can complete an idea map. Follow these steps.

1. Read the paragraph.

2. Check the main idea on the map.

3. Find details about the main idea.

4. Write the details on the idea map.

The Incas were a great people who lived long ago in South America. They built many roads across their lands. They were smart farmers. They were fine artists who made things from gold. The Incas were also good fighters.

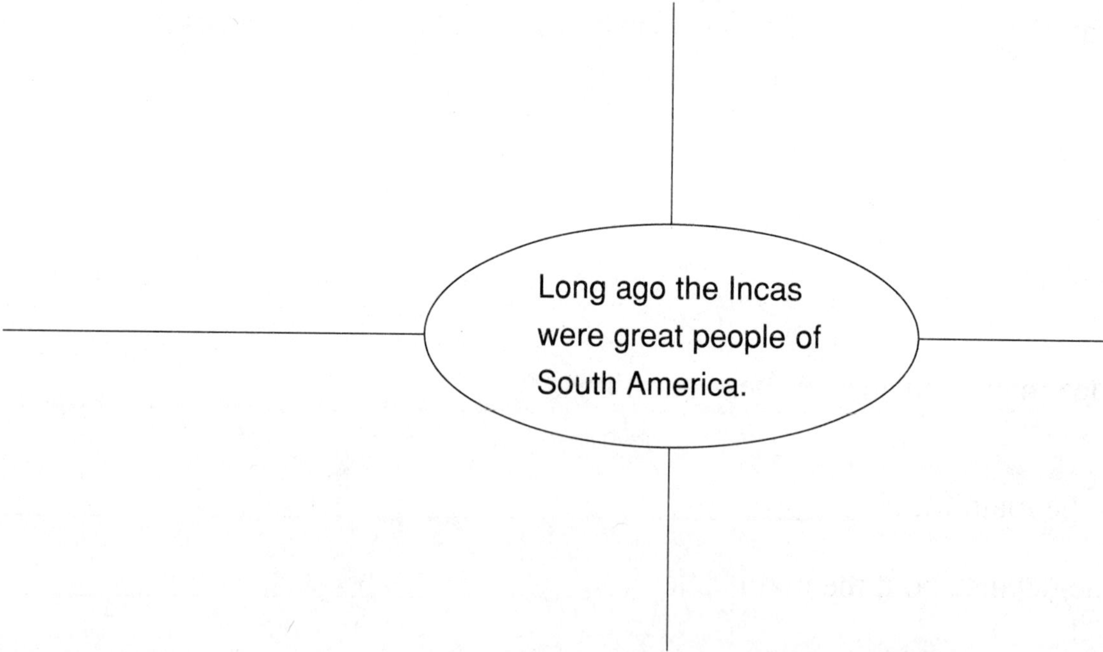

Read this sentence. Does it support the main idea? Explain.

The Incas did not have a written language.

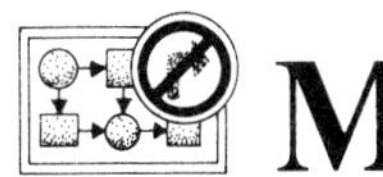 # Mapping It Out

An idea map can also look like the one below. Read the paragraph. Then find the main idea. Write it in the center. Find the details, and write them in the other circles.

Wool is a useful material that comes mainly from sheep. Wool cloth is warm to wear. It does not wrinkle, and it can be cleaned easily. Wool can be made into many kinds of things.

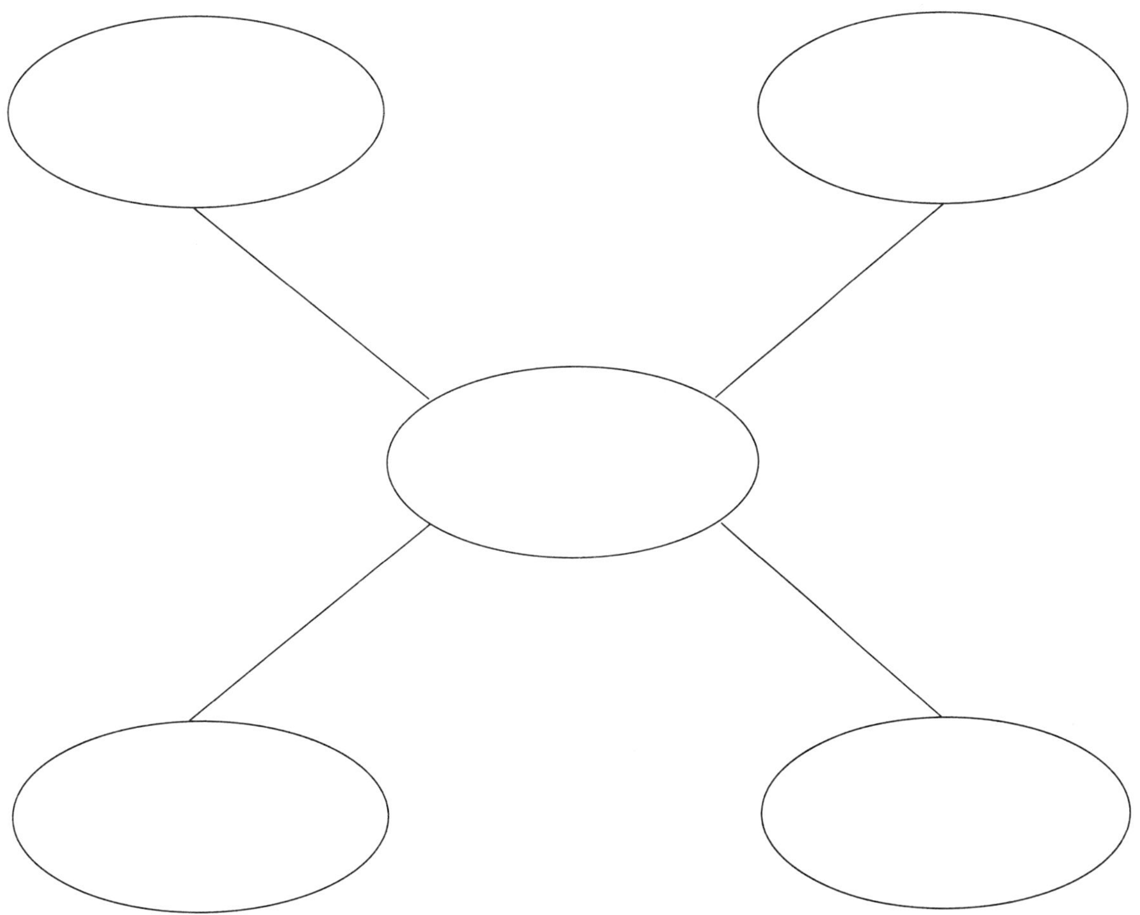

Make up two questions about your idea map. Have a classmate answer them.

Fact Finder

Read this paragraph about salt. Then make an idea map to show the uses of salt.

"Pass the salt," people say. They are going to flavor their food. That is one use of salt. There are many others. Did you know that salt is used in making glass? Salt is also used in making paper, plastic, and soap. Salt helps melt ice and snow in the winter. It is used in some dyes and medicines, too.

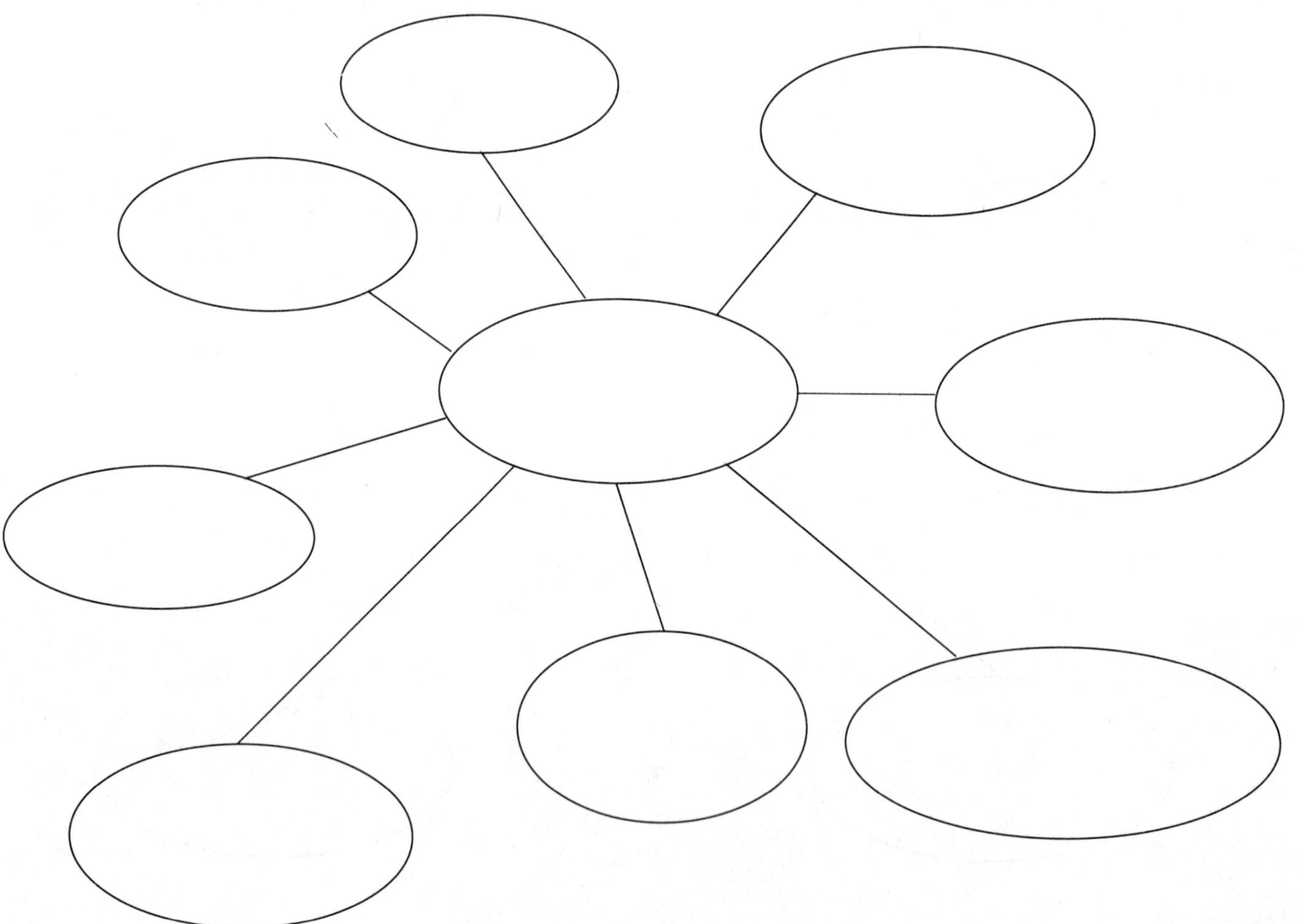

Find out another use for salt. Add it to the map.

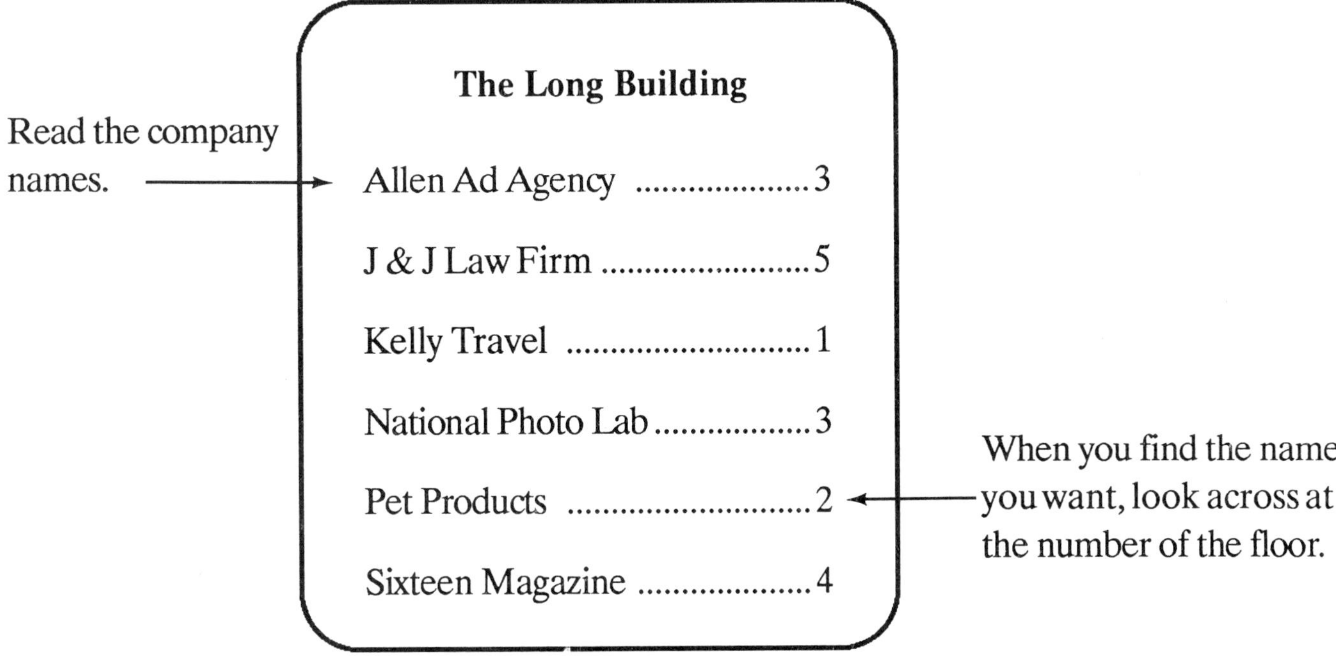 Where Is It?

Imagine this. You go into an office building with many floors. How do you find the office you want?

The answer is easy. You look at the **directory**. A directory is a kind of chart. It tells where things are. This directory lists places in alphabetical order. It tells where different companies are in the same building.

Read the company names. →

The Long Building

Allen Ad Agency 3

J & J Law Firm 5

Kelly Travel 1

National Photo Lab 3

Pet Products ....2 ←

Sixteen Magazine 4

When you find the name you want, look across at the number of the floor.

Now, answer these questions.

1. On what floor is the J & J law Firm? ________________________

2. What company is on the second floor? ________________________

3. Is there a magazine company on the first or the fourth floor? ________________________

4. How many companies are on the third floor? ________________________

What floor would you go to if you were taking a trip? Why?

Mall Map

This is a directory for a shopping mall. The stores are all on one floor. Each store has a different number. This directory lists the stores by what they sell.

MERRY HILLS MALL

Art Supplies

Benson Artists 111

Craft World 103

Books

Bookworm 105

Mystery Mile 100

Treehouse Books 112

Clothing

Caps and Gowns 109

Dawson's Jeans 101

Sport Shop 106

Z.P. Fashions..................... 108

Jewelry

Gold Mine........................ 102

Rings & Things................. 110

Music

Bell Records 104

Study the directory, then answer the questions.

1. What number is Craft World? _______________________________

2. How many jewelry stores are there? _______________________________

3. What store is number 104? _______________________________

4. Where would you go for a mystery book? _______________________________

 How many stores does the mall have altogether?

Step by Step

A picture can show how something happens, step by step.
This kind of picture is a **flow chart**. The flow chart on this
page shows how a butterfly grows.

How a Butterfly Grows

Look at the pictures.

Read each step in order.

1. A butterfly lays eggs.

2. A caterpillar hatches from the eggs.

3. The caterpillar eats and grows.

4. The caterpillar makes a hard cover over its body.

5. A butterfly hatches.

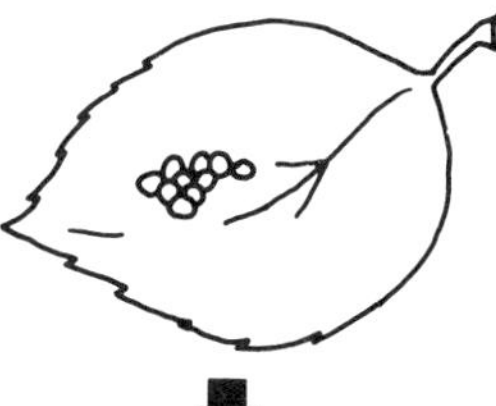
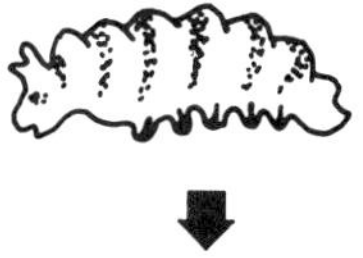

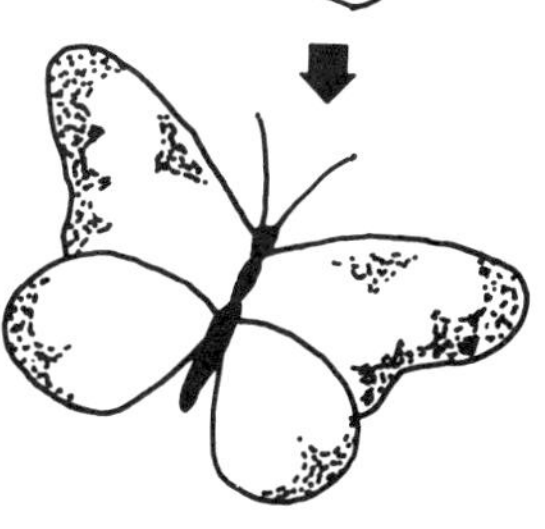

Now, write **True** or **False** next to each statement.

__________ 1. A caterpillar lays eggs.

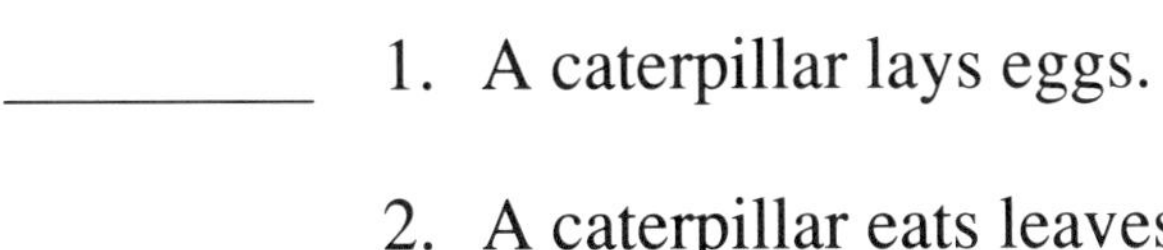

__________ 2. A caterpillar eats leaves.

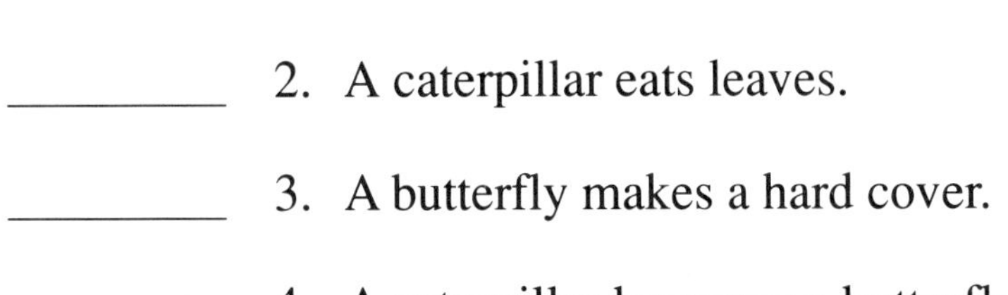

__________ 3. A butterfly makes a hard cover.

__________ 4. A caterpillar becomes a butterfly.

Find out more about the butterfly. What does it eat? How
does it help a garden grow?

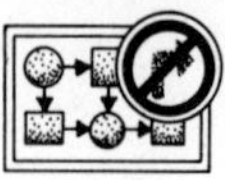# **Follow the Action**

This flow chart shows how to make a bookmark.

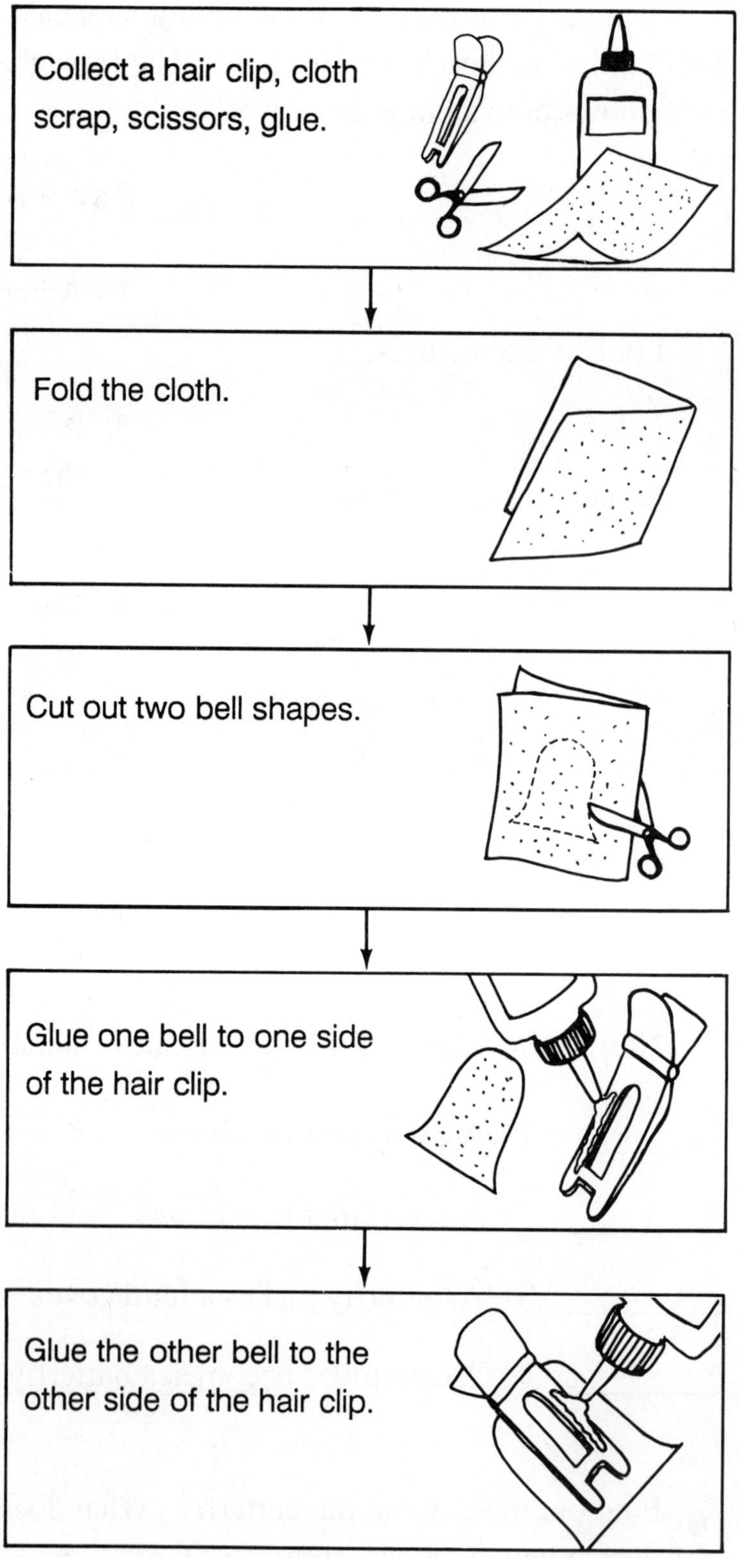

Study the flow chart. Then underline the true statements.

1. Cut the bells out one by one.

2. Glue the bells to the hair clip one by one.

3. Collect the materials you need first.

4. Fold the bells after they are glued.

Follow the flow chart to make your own bookmark.

Collect a hair clip, cloth scrap, scissors, glue.

Fold the cloth.

Cut out two bell shapes.

Glue one bell to one side of the hair clip.

Glue the other bell to the other side of the hair clip.

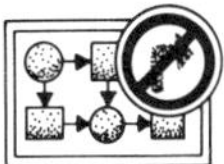

From This to That

This flow chart shows how paper is made.

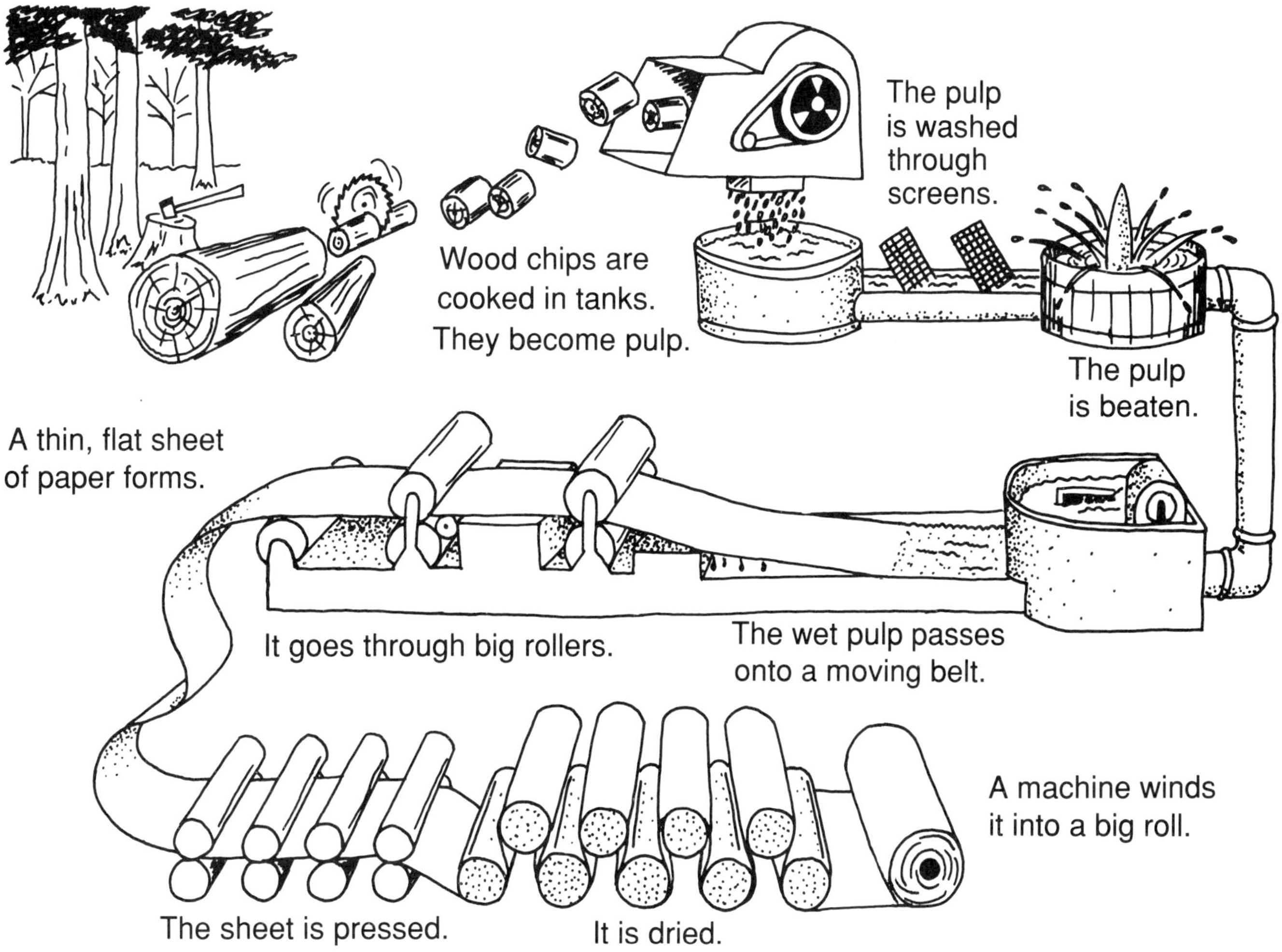

Study the flow chart, then answer the questions.

1. Paper is made from ____ .

2. The cooked chips become ____ .

3. The wet pulp is pressed flat on big____ .

4. Once the paper is pressed, it must be ____ .

Why do you think the pulp goes through screens?

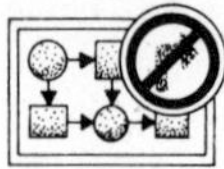

Make it Flow

You can make a flow chart. Tell how to make a gift tag from a greeting card. Follow these steps.

1. Study the picture.

2. Name the materials.

3. Decide what to do.

4. Write the steps in order.

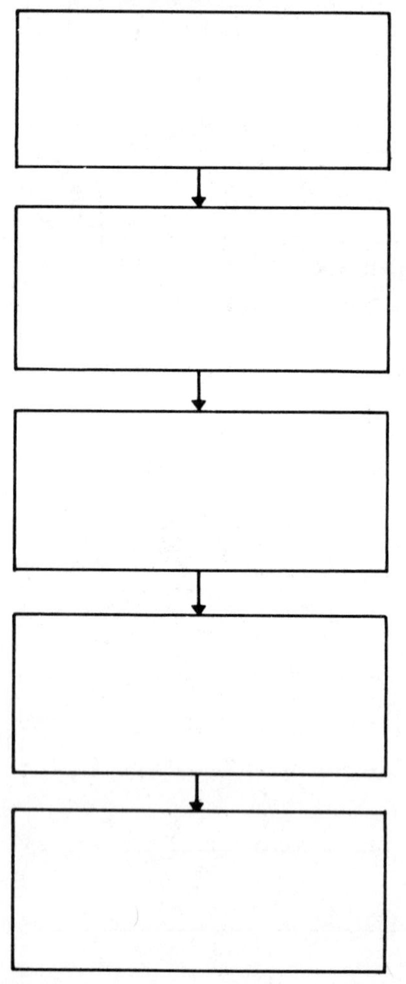

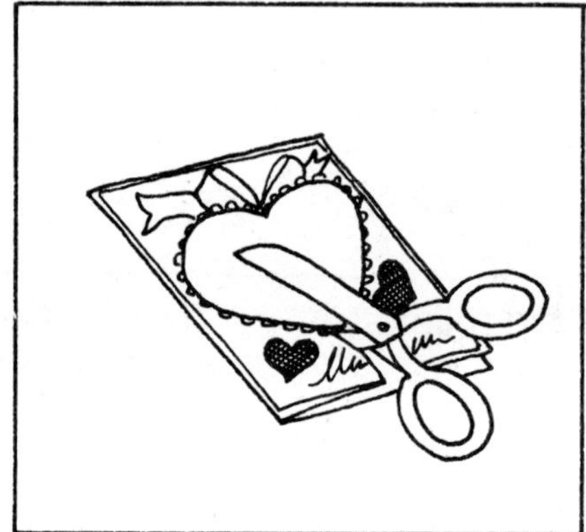

Try following the directions you wrote. Can you improve on them?

Yes Or No?

A computer program is a kind of flow chart. It lists the steps for doing something. When there is a choice, the program asks a "yes or no" question. If the answer is "yes," the computer goes to the next step. If the answer if "no," the computer goes to a different step and tries again.

This flow chart tells how to address an envelope.

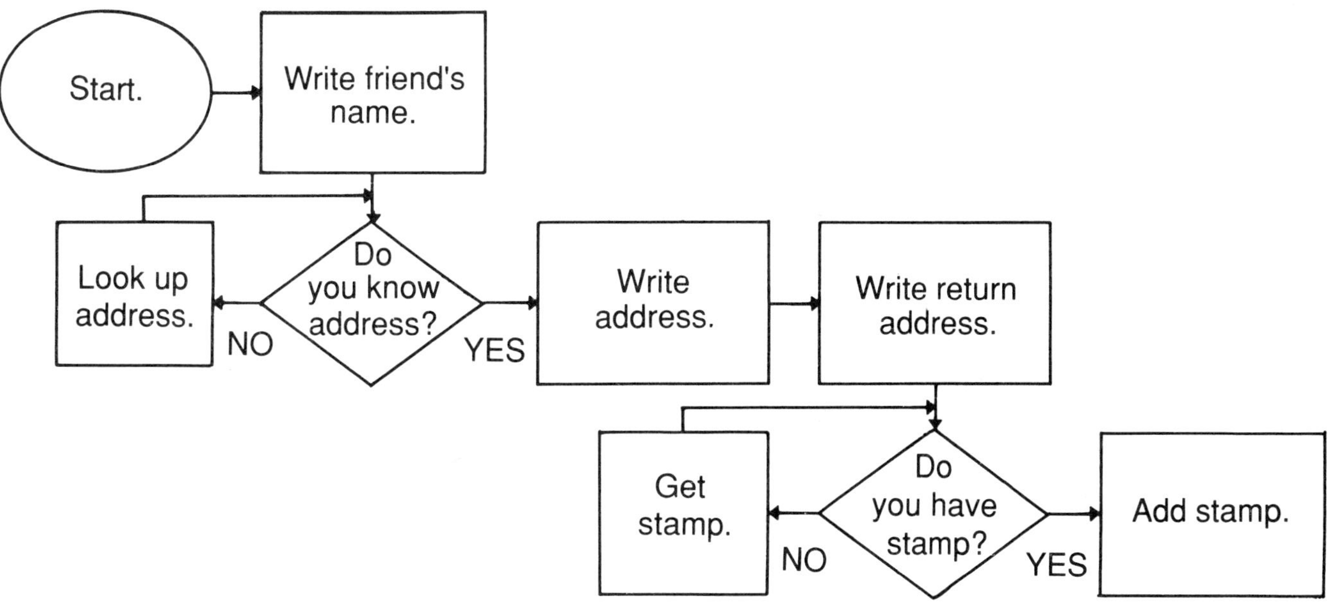

Study the flow chart, then answer the questions.

1. What is the first step? ____

2. What is the first choice you have to make? _______________________________

3. What do you do if you don't know your friend's

   address? ____

4. What do you do after you write the address? _______________________

Tell why each step is important.

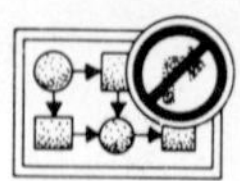 # Give Orders

You can program this computer. Follow these steps. When you are done, your flow chart should tell how to take a telephone message.

1. Read the labels.
2. Decide in what order they go.
3. Write the labels in the flow chart. The triangles are for questions. The boxes are for statements.

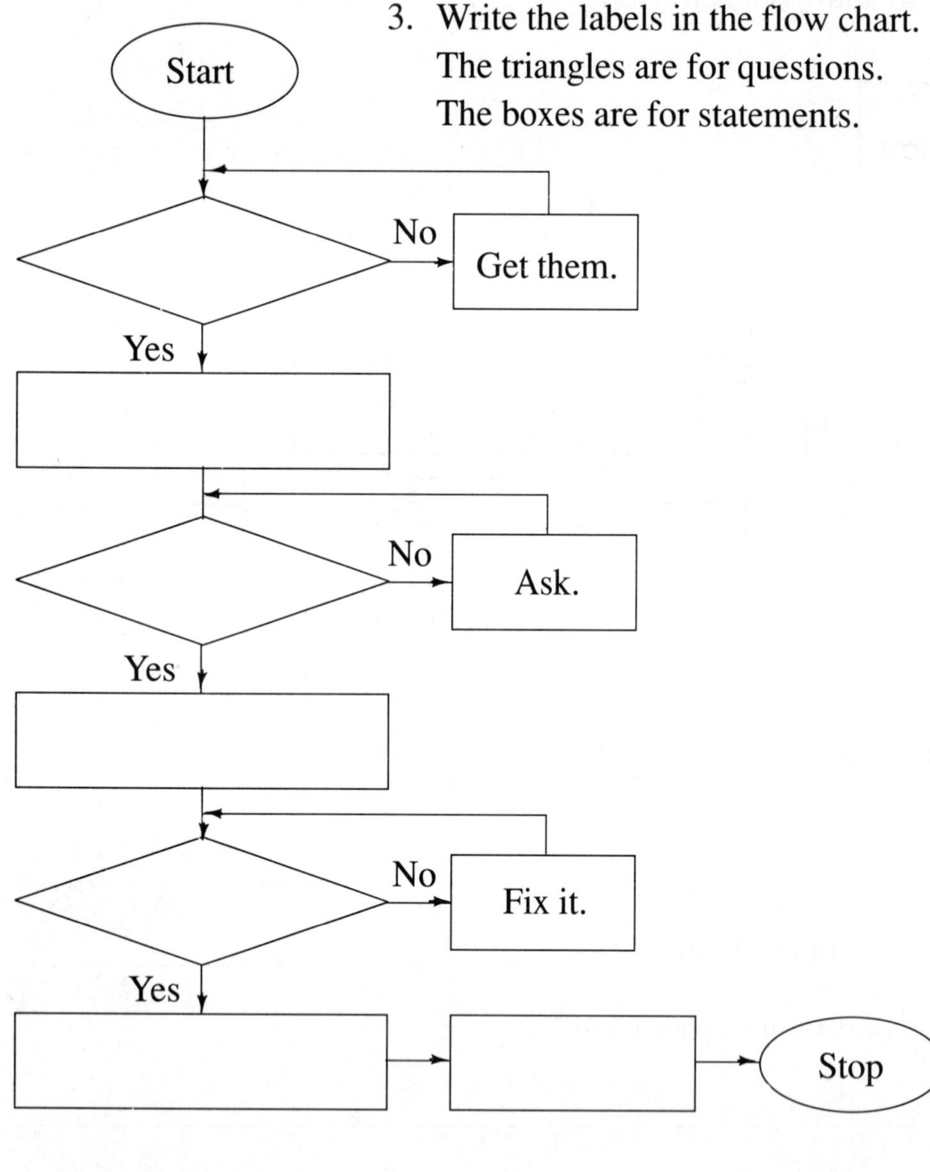

Make up two questions about your computer flow chart. Have a classmate answer them.

In Time

A **time line** shows the order in which things happened. This time line shows when some holidays take place during a year. The first month of the year is January. It is on the left. The last month on the time line is December. It is on the right.

Read the time line from left to right.
Look at the amount of time each part shows.
Read the labels.

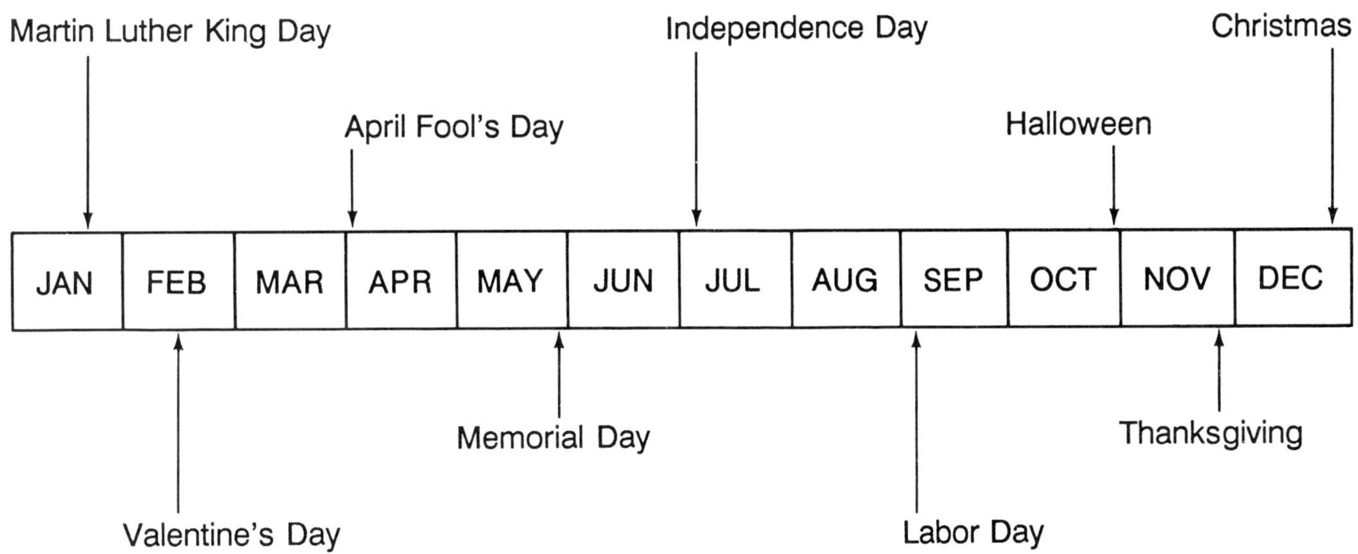

1. What holiday comes in February? _______________________________________

2. In what month is Independence Day? _______________________________________

3. Name an October holiday. _______________________________________

4. Which comes first, Memorial Day or Labor Day? _______________________________________

Which two holidays are closer together, Martin Luther King Day and Christmas, or Martin Luther King Day and April Fool's Day?

Year by Year

This time line shows the events at a school.

Events at North Ridge School

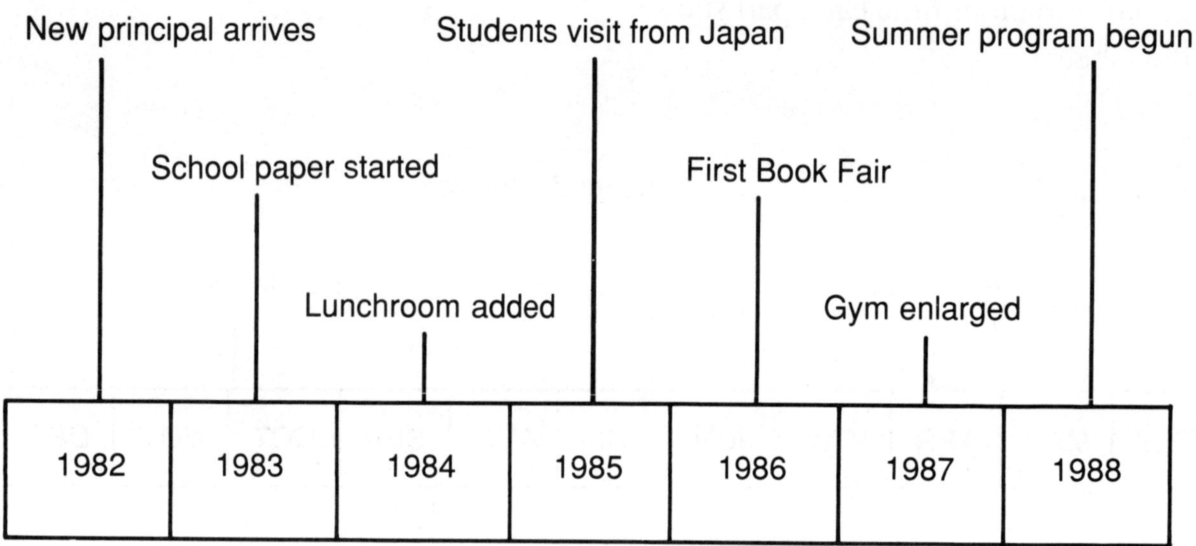

Study the time line, then answer the questions.

1. When was the school paper started? _______________________________

2. What happened in 1985? _______________________________

3. Did the school have its first Book Fair before or after

    the lunchroom was added? _______________________________

4. How many years does the time line cover? _______________________________

Do you think the school had more students in 1988 than in 1982?
Why or why not?

 Diagrams

# History on the Line

A time line can cover many years. Only some of them have labels.

This time line covers 100 years. It tells how a town grew.

History of Pine Woods

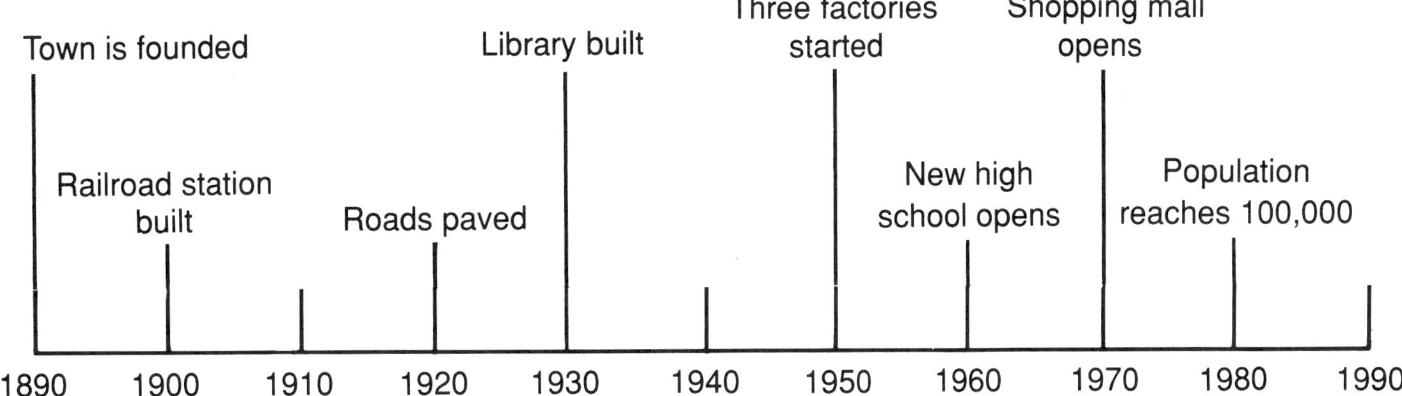

Study the time line, then answer the questions.

1. When were the roads paved? ____

2. What happened in 1950? ____

3. Was the library built before or after the shopping mall? _______________________

4. For about how many years has the town had a railroad

   station? ____

A hospital was built in 1955. Where would you put that on the time line?

Time After Time

Some time lines look like this. The time line on this page shows when different things were invented.

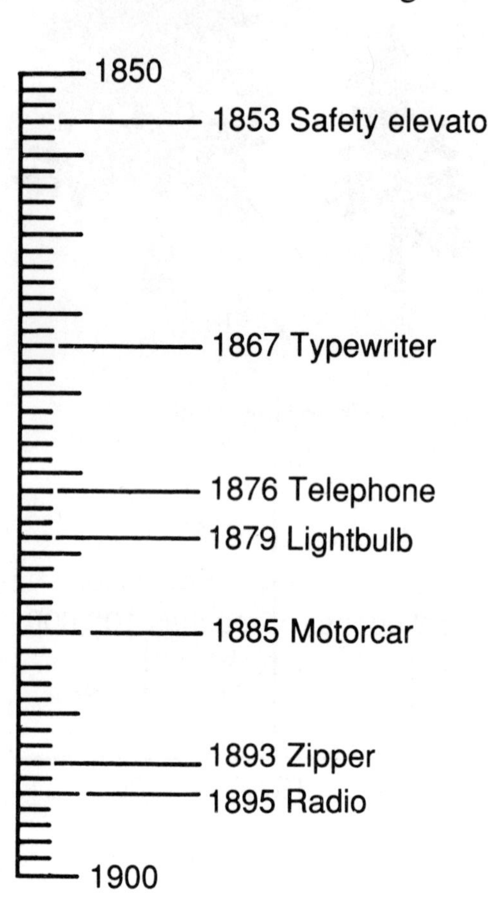

Study the time line, then answer the questions.

1. When was the typewriter invented? _______________________________

2. In what year was the zipper invented? _______________________________

3. What was invented in 1876? _______________________________

4. About how long ago was the motorcar invented? _______________________________

Think about one of these inventions. How did it change peoples' lives?

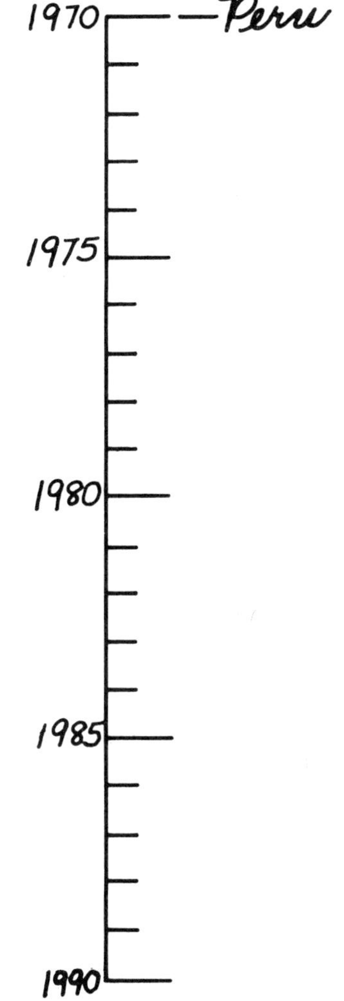 Shaky Times

You can add facts to a time line. These facts tell when some big earthquakes happened. The first earthquake is already on the time line. Follow the steps for the rest.

1. Read the facts.

2. Count the lines to find the year on the time line.

3. Write the year and the country on the time line.

Earthquake Facts

Peru, 1970
Iran, 1972
China, 1976
Romania, 1977
Iran, 1978
Yemen, 1982
Mexico, 1985
Ecuador, 1987

Now, answer these questions.

1. In what year did China have an earthquake? _______________________

2. What country had an earthquake in 1985? _______________________

3. Name two years in which Iran had earthquakes. _______________________

Find each country on a map.

Name ____

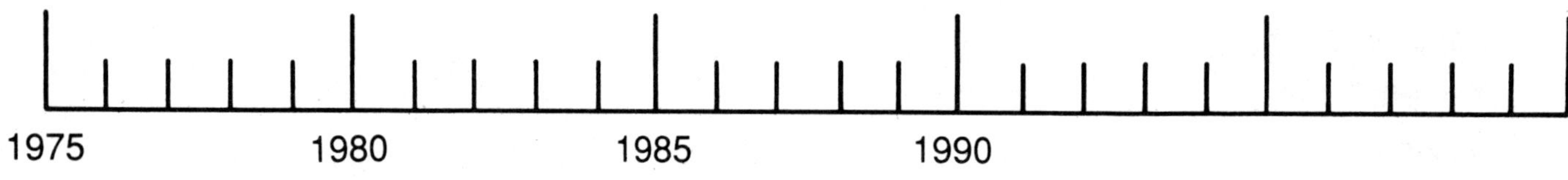

Your Life Time

You can make a time line. Follow these steps.

1. Write down five or six important events in your life.

2. Put the events in order.

3. Find the place where each event will go on the timeline.

4. Write the events on the time line.

1975   1980   1985   1990

Write three questions about your time line. Have a
classmate answer them.

1.____

2.____

3.____

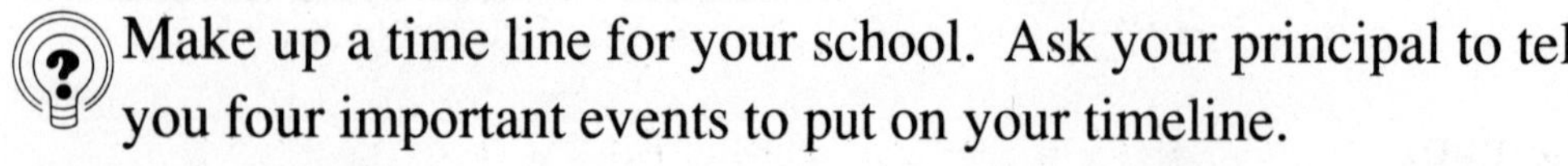

Make up a time line for your school. Ask your principal to tell
you four important events to put on your timeline.

Some Symbols

A **symbol** is a picture with a special meaning. You already know many symbols.

Study the symbol box. Then draw the correct symbol next to each sentence.

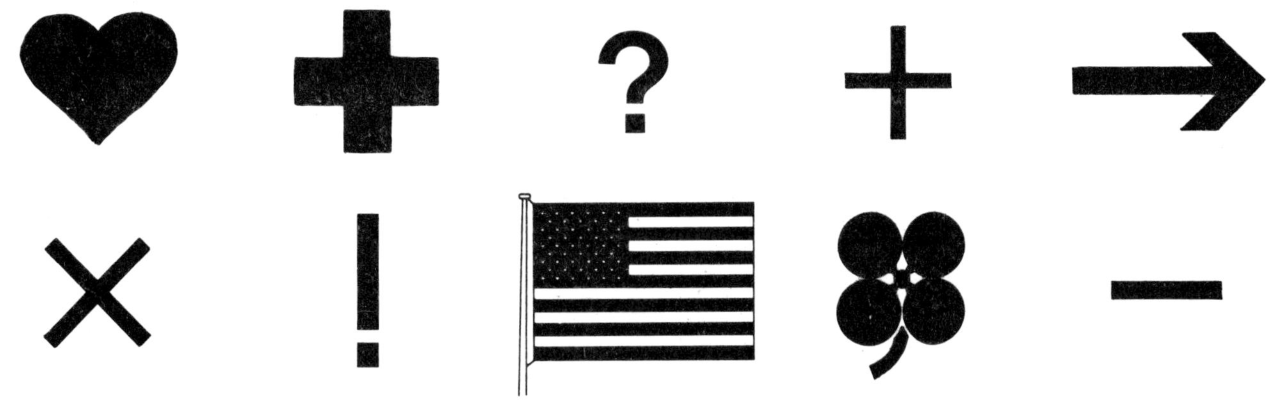

__________________ 1. I am used in math. I tell you to add.

__________________ 2. I show strong feeling at the end of a sentence.

__________________ 3. I stand for love. You use me on Valentine's Day.

__________________ 4. I am a lucky symbol. You see me on St. Patrick's Day.

__________________ 5. I am a math symbol. I tell you to subtract.

__________________ 6. I am a first aid symbol. I mean that help is near.

__________________ 7. I show that a sentence is a question.

__________________ 8. I tell you to multiply. You use me in math.

__________________ 9. I am a symbol of the United States. You salute me.

__________________ 10. I am a helpful symbol. I tell you which way to look or go.

Make up a symbol of your own. Tell what it stands for.

Introducing Symbols   ◾ ◀ 49 ▶ ◾   **Diagrams**

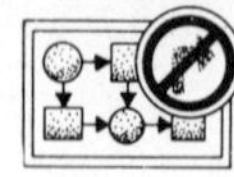

Some More Symbols

Study the symbols below. Then put the correct symbol in front of each sentence.

________________ 1. I warn you of poison!

________________ 2. I am a math symbol. I mean "divide."

________________ 3. I am a symbol of peace.

________________ 4. I am a religious symbol.

________________ 5. I am a symbol of plenty.

________________ 6. I stand for a dollar.

________________ 7. I set off words that people say.

________________ 8. I am a musical symbol.

________________ 9. I mean "equal to."

________________ 10. I stand for cents.

Choose three signs. Give an example of how you would use them.

Symbols Say

In some languages symbols stand for words or ideas. Below are some Indian symbols and their meanings.

Study the symbols. Then read them. Write the story in English on the lines.

____

____

____

____

____

Write a title for the story.

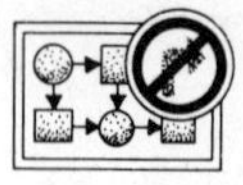

Signs and Symbols

Many signs have symbols. Symbols are easy to read. They
are handy when people don't speak the same language.
Match these signs with their meanings.

1.    _______   a. Deer cross here.

2.    _______   b. There is a public phone here.

3.    _______   c. You can get food here.

4.    _______   d. This is a bike path.

5.    _______   e. Children cross here.

6.    _______   f. This is a wheelchair ramp.

7.    _______   g. This is a picnic area.

8.    _______   h. There is a railroad crossing here.

 Which symbols are important for safety?

Name ______________________________

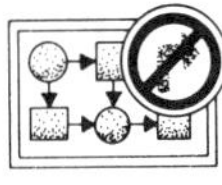

Follow the Signs

Signs have different uses. Some give orders. These signs are usually in circles. A line across a symbol on these signs means "no" or "not allowed." Other signs give warnings. These signs are usually in diamonds or triangles.

Study these signs. Write what each means.

1. ______________________________

2. ______________________________

3. ______________________________

4. ______________________________

5. ______________________________

6. ______________________________

7. ______________________________

8. ______________________________

9. ______________________________

Draw a sign that means "No Dogs Allowed."

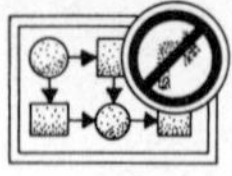 # At the Airport

Your family has landed at an airport and has some extra time between planes. How well can you find your way around? Read the signs. Match each one to a sentence on page 55.

a.  b.  c. 

d.  e.  f. 

g.  h.  i. 

j.  k.  l. 

At the Airport

Which sign will help? Write the letter of the correct sign from page 54 next to each sentence.

____________ 1. Passengers who have just landed want to pick up their bags.

____________ 2. Your father must make a business call.

____________ 3. Your brother needs a restroom.

____________ 4. Your mother has to change your baby sister's diaper.

____________ 5. Someone asks where to find a bus to the city.

____________ 6. You are looking for a place to buy a magazine.

____________ 7. Your family would like a snack.

____________ 8. Your family wants to get to the lower level of the airport.

____________ 9. Your mother wants to find out when your plane will leave.

____________ 10. Your brother loses his teddy bear.

____________ 11. You pass some doors that are closed to the public.

____________ 12. Your father wants to mail a postcard to your grandmother.

 Why are these signs useful in an international airport?

Getting the Message

A **news cartoon** is a comment on an event or problem in the news. The cartoon shows what the artist thinks. The artist uses pictures and words to get the message across. Words at the bottom of a news cartoon are called **captions.** This news cartoon has a message about some problems in the news.

Study the cartoon.

Read the caption.

I thought you could solve anything!

Now, answer these questions.

1. What problems did the scientist want the computer to solve? ______________________

   ____

2. What did the computer say for each problem? ______________________________

   ____

3. Why is the scientist upset? ____

Why can't the computer solve the problems?

Point of View

This news cartoon has a comment about transportation.

I hear it's a red light in Boston!

Study the news cartoon, then answer the questions.

1. Who is talking? ____

2. Where are the people? ____

3. What is the problem? ____

   ____

4. How does the artist stretch the truth? ____

   ____

What is the artist saying about traffic problems?

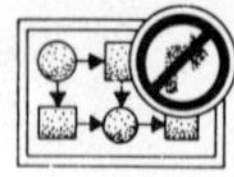

Cartoon Comment

This news cartoon is about a problem in some professional sports.

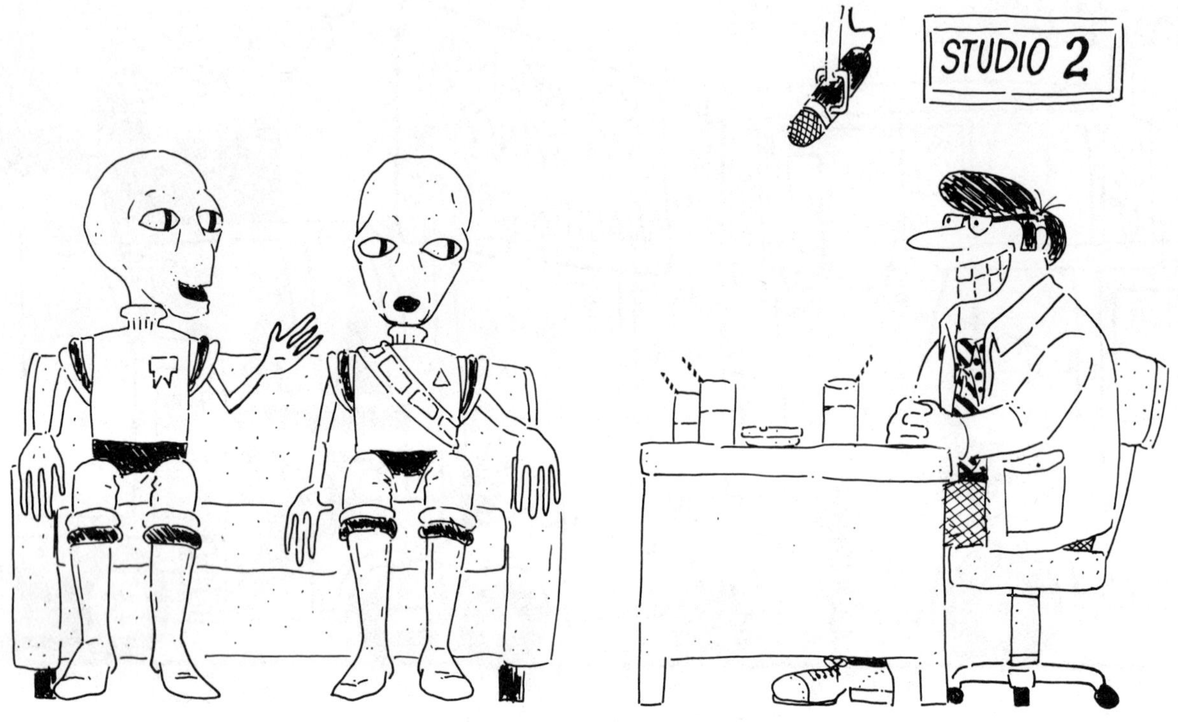

We enjoy your sports. They are much like the wars we fight on our planet.

Study the news cartoon, then answer the questions.

1. Who is the man in this cartoon? _______________________________________

2. Where are the visitors from? ____

3. Who is speaking? ____

4. What are sports being compared to? __________________________________

   Why? ____

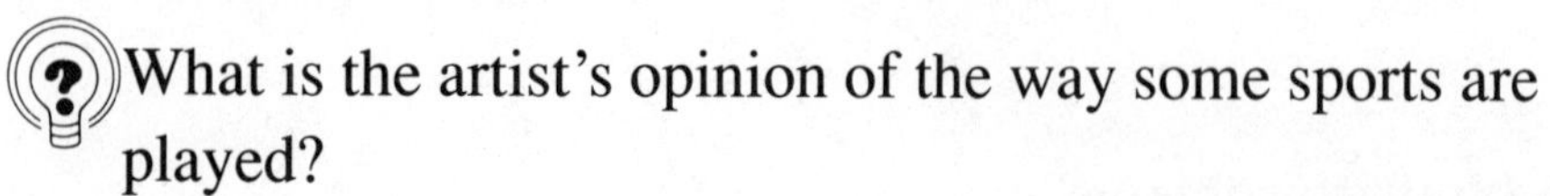What is the artist's opinion of the way some sports are played?

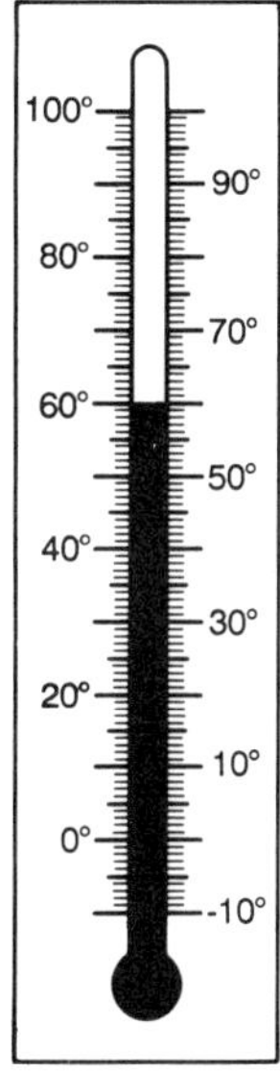

Hot or Cold?

This is a picture of a **thermometer**. It is a tool for measuring temperature. A red line rises to what the temperature is. The higher the line goes, the warmer the temperature. This thermometer measures in degrees F (for Fahrenheit). It shows a temperature of 60 degrees.

You can write sixty degrees like this: 60°.

Mark each thermometer to show what the temperature is. Use a red pencil.

1. 40°F
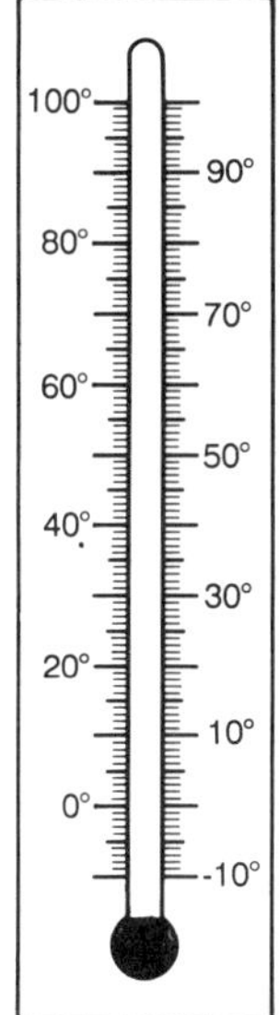

2. 75°F
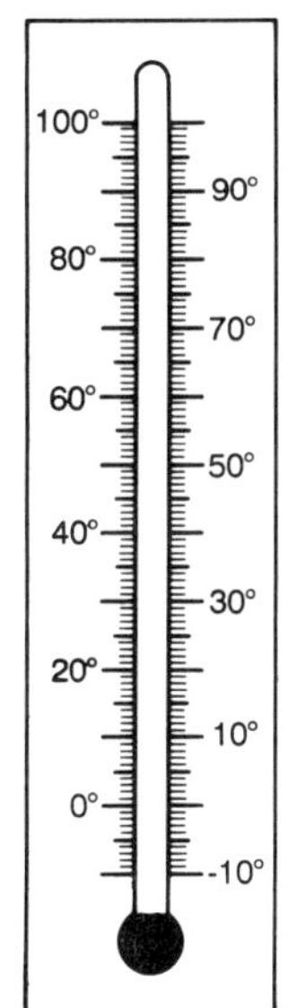

3. 90°F
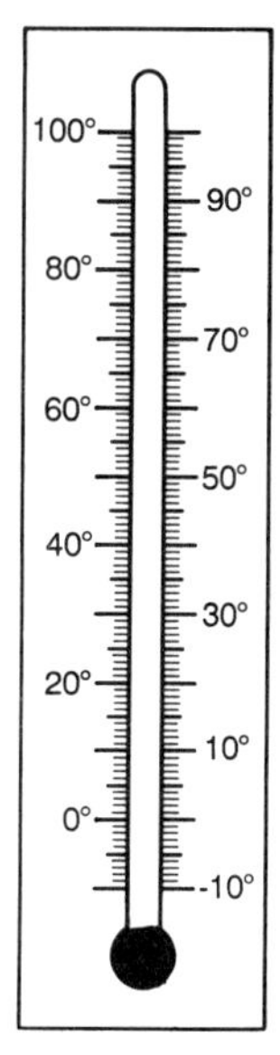

4. 18°F
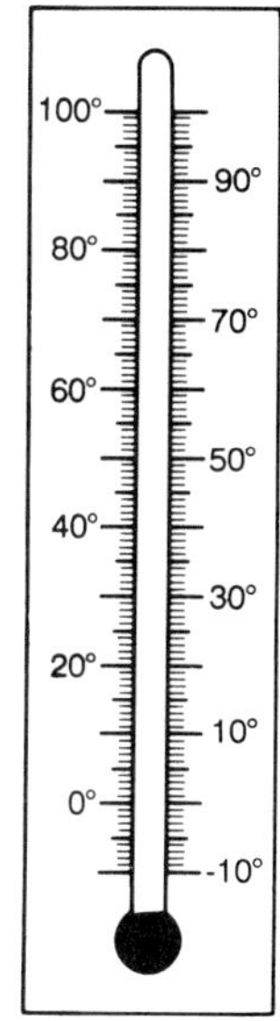

Answer these questions.

5. Which temperature is the hottest? ___________________

6. Which temperature is the coldest? ___________________

Choose two temperatures on this page. Tell how you would dress to go outside in each temperature.

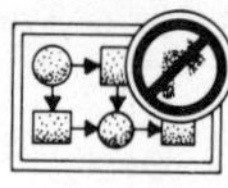 # Weather Wise

Study these thermometers. Then read each statement.
Decide which temperature best matches each statement. Then
write the letter next to the statement.

a. 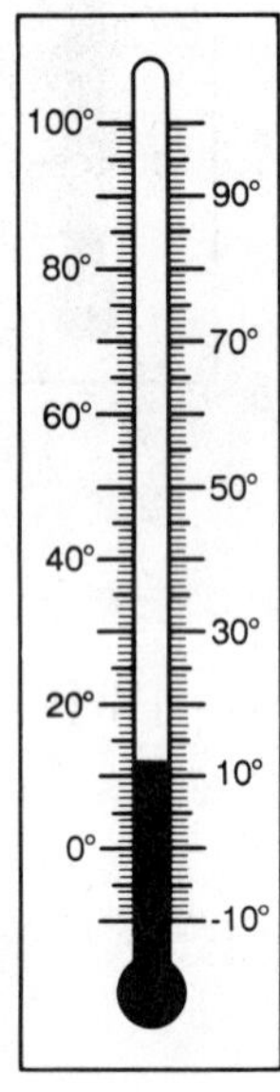   b. 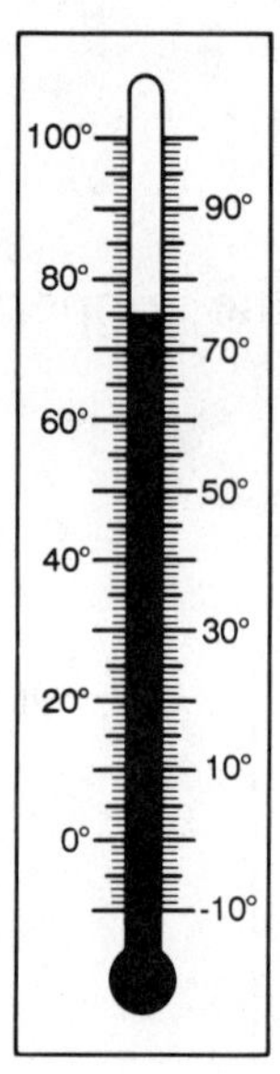   c. 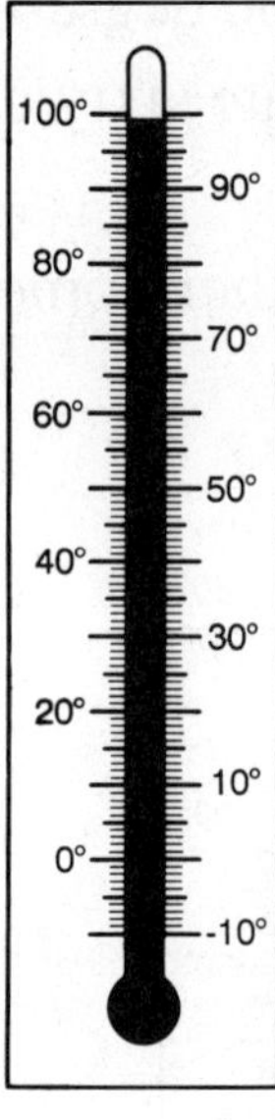

___________ 1. It's too hot to do anything. Stay inside and turn on the
air conditioner.

___________ 2. What a beautiful day! The temperature is perfect.

___________ 3. Today it is really cold. Don't go outside unless you
have to.

___________ 4. This is a good day for the beach. A swim in the cool
water will feel good.

___________ 5. What a perfect day for a long bicycle ride!

___________ 6. Bundle up! This is winter weather.

 What other things besides temperature affect what you wear
and what you do?

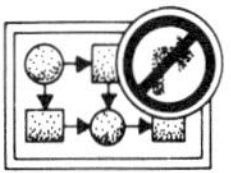

Vocabulary Fun

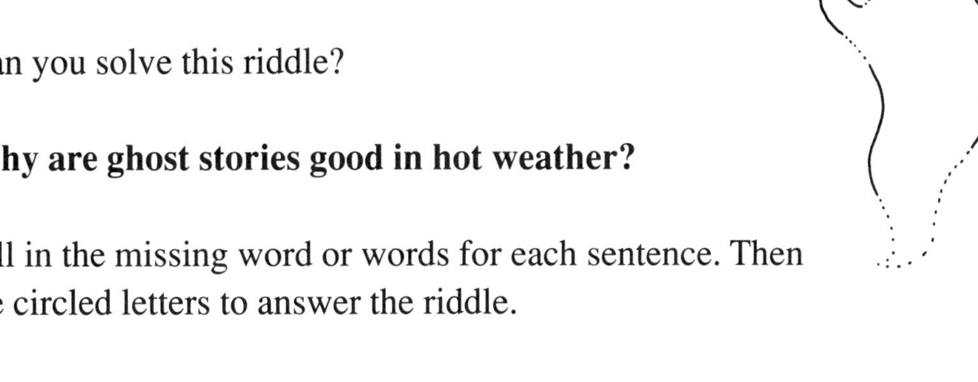

Can you solve this riddle?

Why are ghost stories good in hot weather?

Fill in the missing word or words for each sentence. Then use the circled letters to answer the riddle.

1. A set of pictures that shows the steps for making or doing something is called a

   — — — — — — — — — ◯ —

2. An — — — — — — — — — — — — —

   — ◯ — — — shows how something is arranged or set up.

3. You can find out where places in an office building are by reading the

   — — — ◯ — — — — — — .

4. A drawing that shows the inside of something is called a

   — — — — — — ◯ diagram.

5. A drawing with labels that shows the parts of something is a

   — — ◯ — — — — .

6. The arrangement of rooms in a house can be shown on a

   — — — — ◯ — — — — — .

7. You can show how facts are related on an — — ◯ — map.

8. An artists comments on events and problems in a — — — ◯

   — — — — — — — .

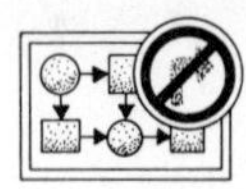

Vocabulary Fun

9. The words under a news cartoon are called the

— — — — — ◯ — .

10. A flow chart with circles, diamonds, and boxes is for a

◯ — — — — — — — — .

11. A tool for measuring temperature is a

— ◯ — — — — — — — — — — .

12. A fact that supports the main idea on a map is a

— — — — ◯ — .

13. A — — — — ◯ — — —

shows the order in which things happened over a period of time.

14. A picture that stands for something is a — — — — — ◯ .

15. When you make a guess about what will happen next, you

— — — — ◯ — — the outcome.

16. Many — — — ◯ — have symbols on them.

17. A thermometer measures heat in — — ◯ — — — — .

— — — — — — — — — — — — — — — — — —

page 27
Check to be sure that students name some of the castle's features as shown by the floor plan.

page 28
1. Party Chairman; 2. Food Planner; 3. Decorations Planner; 4. Food Planner, Decorations Planner, Games Planner; or, Food Helpers, Decorations Helpers *The committee will organize a party.

page 29
Alabama; Massachusetts; Idaho; Mississippi; Connecticut; Ohio * Possible answers: Wisconsin, North and South Dakota, Michigan

page 30
1. big fish; 2. small fish; 3. tiny sea animals; 4. tiny sea animals *People would go on top of the big fish.

page 31
1. Farmer John has a vegetable garden. 2. peas, carrots, beans, corn; 3. no *Add another line and write beets on it.

page 32
Details should include: built many roads; were smart farmers; were fine artists; were good fighters. *The sentence does not support the main idea because it tells about something that the Incas lacked.

page 33
Main Idea: Wool is useful material from sheep. Details: warm to wear; doesn't wrinkle; cleans easily; can be made into many things.

page 34
Main Idea: Salt has many uses. Details: flavor food; make glass; make paper; make plastic; make soap; melt ice and snow; used in dyes; used in medicines *Possible answers: Salt is used in food processing.

page 35
1. 5; 2. Pet Products; 3. fourth; 4. two *first floor (Kelly Travel)

page 36
1. 103; 2. two; 3. Bell Records; 4. Mystery Mile *twelve

page 37
False; 2. True; 3. False; 4. True *Butterflies eat the nectar from flowers. They carry the pollen from flower to flower to help the garden grow.

page 38
Students should underline sentences 2 and 3. 1. Check to be sure students have followed the steps in the flow chart to make the bookmark.

page 39
1. wood chips; 2. pulp; 3. rollers; 4. dried *The screens sift out impurities.

page 40
Check to be sure that students write steps that tell reader to collect old greeting card, scissors, hole punch, yarn pen; cut out a picture from the card; tell reader to punch a hole for the string; tell reader to attach the string or yarn; and tell reader to print TO and FROM on the gift tag.

page 41
1. Write friend's name. 2. Do you know the address? 3. You look it up. 4. Write the return address. *Each step is necessary to be sure the letter gets to the receiver, or back to the sender if there is a problem with delivery.

page 42
The labels should be written in this order: Do you have a pencil and pad? Write down the caller's name. Can you spell it? Write down message. Is message correct? Say good-bye. Hang up.

page 43
1. Valentine's Day; 2. July; 3. Halloween; 4. Memorial Day *Martin Luther King Day and Christmas

page 44
1. 1983; 2. Students from Japan visited. 3. after; 4. seven *It probably had more in 1988 because the gym was enlarged and a summer program was begun.

page 45
1. 1920; 2. Three factories were started. 3. before; 4. about 90 *between 1950 and 1960

page 46
1. 1867; 2. 1893; 3. telephone; 4. about 100 years ago *Students should recognize that the invention made life easier, improved communication or transportation, or in the case of the elevator, made tall buildings possible.

page 47
Check to see that students place country names and dates on the time line accurately. 1. 1976; 2. Mexico; 3. 1972, 1978

page 48
Check to be sure students place events sequentially and accurately on the time line.

page 49
1. plus sign; 2. exclamation mark; 3. heart; 4. clover; 5. minus sign; 6. cross; 7. question mark; 8. multiplication sign; 9. flag; 10. arrow

page 50
1. skull; 2. division sign; 3. dove; 4. cross; 5. cornucopia; 6. dollar sign; 7. quotation marks; 8. musical note; 9. equal sign; 10. cent sign

page 51
Line one: A chief is on a long journey. Line two: The chief has wisdom and strength. Line three: The chief's journey takes him through a desert. Line four: The chief sees a good sign. Line five: The chief does a dance because he found game.

page 52
1. f; 2. e; 3. a; 4. b; 5. h; 6. d; 7. g; 8. c *the crossing symbols

page 53
1. No Smoking; 2. Slippery When Wet; 3. No Left Turn; 4. No Parking; 5. People Crossing; 6. Sharp Curve; 7. No Trucks; 8. Traffic Light Ahead; 9. Tractor Crossing *Students' sign should have a line across it.

pages 54 - 55
1. d; 2. l; 3. f; 4. c; 5. i; 6. e; 7. b; 8. j; 9. h; 10. a; 11. g; 12. k *People who speak different languages can all understand pictures.

page 56
1. hunger, crime, pollution, disease, war; 2. ????; 3. He thought the computer could solve anything. *The problems have to do with human nature.

page 57
1. lady in a car; 2. in cars and trucks on a highway; 3. a huge traffic jam; 4. by suggesting that a red light in Boston would cause a holdup in Washington, D.C. *The artist suggests that they are severe and need attention before they get to this point.

page 58
1. a talk show host; 2. another planet; outer space; 3. one of the aliens; 4. Sports are being compared to war because of the belligerent way in which they are sometimes played. *The artist is making the point that some sports in America are too rough and dangerous.

page 59
1 - 4. Check to be sure students draw red lines that mark 40, 75, 90, and 18 degrees. 5. 90 degrees; 6. 18 degrees *Students should indicate lightweight clothing for the high temperatures, and warm clothing for the cold ones.

page 60
1. c; 2. b; 3. a; 4. c; 5. b; 6. a *Possible answers: wind, humidity, precipitation

pages 61-62
1. flow chart; 2. organization chart; 3. directory; 4. cutaway; 5. diagram; 6. floor plan; 7. idea; 8. news cartoon; 9. caption; 10. computer; 11. thermometer; 12. detail; 13. time line; 14. symbol; 15. predict; 16. signs; 17. degrees
Riddle Answer: They are so chilling!